My Life on the Rock

My Life on the Rock

A Rebel Returns
to the Catholic Faith

Jeff Cavins

ASCENSION
P R E S S

Ascension Press, L.L.C.
Post Office Box 1990
West Chester PA 19380
Ordering: (800) 376-0520
www.AscensionPress.com

Cover design by Kinsey Advertising, Huntington Beach, California

04 05 04 03 02

Printed in the United States of America
ISBN 0–9659228–3–9

Contents

To Robert and Trish Cavins
and Andreas and Alice Tobler

If God goes in search of man, created in His own image and likeness, He does so because He loves him eternally in the Word, and wishes to raise him in Christ to the dignity of an adoptive son. God therefore goes in search of man who *is His special possession* in a way unlike any other creature. Man is God's possession by virtue of a choice made in love: God seeks man out, moved by His fatherly heart.

— Pope John Paul II
Tertio Millennio Adveniente

Acknowledgements

I would like to thank Mark Shea for assisting me in organizing my thoughts throughout the writing of this book. Mark familiarized himself with my entire story, then gave me invaluable advice that allowed me to stand back and see the story as a whole. I could not have done this without him. I would like to thank Scott Hahn who repeatedly reminded me that this story needed to be written. He has become the brother I never had. While on my journey back to the Church, I viewed a video of the Holy Father, John Paul II's visit to Denver. As I watched the video I was profoundly moved by the smile of a young teenage girl. I don't know who she is, but her smile reduced me to tears when I saw her admiration for the Vicar of Christ. Whoever you are . . . thank you! Throughout the writing of this book I have been inspired by the writings of Thomas Howard, who I believe is — and will go down in history as — one of the truly great writers of our time. Finally, I consider my lovely wife Emily to be co-author of this book. Not only is she my best friend, but her love, personality, prayers, and faithfulness are printed within every paragraph of my life. She contributed many hours, working hard to ensure the integrity of the story.

Searching in St. Hubert's

I sat in the balcony looking down the single aisle toward the old altar and tabernacle of St. Hubert's Catholic Church in Chanhassen, Minnesota. On each side of the front of the church were statues with stands of candles flickering nearby, which comforted me somehow. Intently I studied each statue, hoping and praying they would twitch or something. At eighteen, I had heard reports that sometimes statues cried or did other strange things, so I was anticipating a similar sign that would let me know I'd made contact with God.

To look at me, sitting there in the choir loft and silently contemplating the statues, no one would have thought I was in the midst of a serious spiritual search, not even the priest who occasionally walked through the sanctuary, unaware of my presence. No one was aware of my hunger for God, not my parents, nor my girlfriend, Karen, nor even my best friend, Randy.

I was the average American Catholic boy. I had grown up in the western suburbs of Minneapolis, Minnesota, attending weekly Mass and holy days of obligation. We went to confession as a family several times per year. I had a giant black rosary, but I don't recall using it for prayer, however as a boy it had made a terrific set of reins for my imaginary horse at the end of my bed. I also wore a scapular for a while, but I didn't know what it meant or what it was for. And I once had a little children's Mass book I had received for first Communion and I used to take it

with me to church. But, again, I didn't really know what
it was all about and I eventually lost it. My parents were
devoted to seeing that I and my younger sisters, Jayne and
Leslie, would ourselves embrace the Catholic Faith. They
were founding members of a new church in Bloomington,
Minnesota, which was pastored by Fr. Paul Dudley. While
my parents didn't pass on a lot of content about the Faith,
I was aware by listening to my mother's side of the family
that leaving the Church was not a good thing. I had a
general sense that what we believed was the "real McCoy"
and I needn't look further. I once attended a Lutheran service with a friend and discovered how opposed my parents
were to that venture.

As a boy I was fascinated with church, especially the
tabernacle behind the altar. I was drawn to it and liked
to just sit near it. I had served as an altar boy occasionally and always tried to peer inside the tabernacle. In an
inexplicable way, it brought a warmth and a comfort that
I couldn't articulate.

When I was fourteen, we moved to a new home in Chanhassen about fifteen miles further west. Though I was still
intrigued by the mysterious holiness of the Church, a move
to a new parish left me less inspired than I had been as a boy.
I lost contact with Fr. Dudley and most of my friends from
Bloomington. Instead, my attention began to turn toward
typical teenage concerns: girls, motorcycles, and sports.

I was an odd combination of athlete, intense reader, and
comedian. I discovered I was a fast runner after an incident
in my Bloomington neighborhood. I came across several
boys from my school attacking the neighbor girl on her
way home. They were trying to pull her tights off, much
to their amusement. I was enraged that they would pick
on her so I pulled the boys off her and shouted at her to

run. She did run off, so now the boys turned upon me their collective urge to beat someone up. In junior high I was smaller than most of the kids, and after that incident I became the target of that gang's revenge. It became a daily experience to try to outwit or outrun those boys. To get home I had to cross a small bridge over a creek secluded by trees. If I didn't get over the bridge before they reached it, they would beat me up. I was helpless against them. When they did catch me I would roll up in a ball and let them kick me and call me names until they tired of it.

I discovered by this mad dash to get home that I enjoyed sprinting and running, so throughout junior high and high school I was on the track team. I ran sprints as well as cross-country and came up the winner most of the time.

One of my great passions was reading. When I was in sixth grade, my teacher, Mr. Knight, really hooked me on books. He had given me a copy of *Robinson Crusoe* and it launched me into a lifetime of voracious reading. At first my dad would buy me books, but after I devoured them so quickly he decided he'd pay half. I would mow lawns in the summer and shovel driveways in the winter in order to earn money to buy books. One book I read over and over was *My Side of the Mountain* by Jean Craighead George. It was about a boy who went to the Catskill Mountains and lived in a tree. The hero of the story would go into the city to get books and then return to his tree to read and think in peace. Influenced by this book, I used to take a backpack with books, a package of beef jerky, and a rotisserie chicken from the nearby convenience store out into a forested park where I'd rough it . . . until dinnertime. Books drew me into worlds beyond my own. I didn't realize that most of the kids my age were not quite so interested in reading.

My idea of a good time was inviting someone to spend the night in order to sit up late and read. I couldn't figure out why they didn't like my idea.

My love of books and love for words moved me to be interested in journalism and broadcasting. I used to beg my dad to take me to radio stations so I could watch the DJs. I would go to the state fair and just sit for hours outside the broadcast booths. As I looked toward college, this was the route I wanted to take. For this to take place I had a few insecurities to overcome first. One of them was speaking in front of people. The first time I ever stood up in front of a group was at camp in seventh grade. All I had to do was read the Lord's Prayer, but when I stood behind the podium, I looked up at my fellow campers, fell over backward, and promptly passed out. Eventually I realized, if I could make people laugh, I would not be so afraid of standing up in front of my peers. I learned this in high school on a dare from my best friend Randy Kerber, who was on the speech team. He dared me to go out for speech as he had once dared me to go out for the hockey team. I had taken him up on the hockey dare and had become the starting goalie, so I figured, "Why not give this a try?" So I attempted a forensic speech competition . . . with less illustrious results.

The first meet was supposed to be a public recitation of serious poetry. I prepared myself, had the poem completely memorized, stepped up in front of the judges, and gave the introduction.

Then I blanked. Where the poem had once been stored in my brain there was just a message reading "file erased."

So I went back and gave the introduction again.

Then I cleared my throat, blinked, and tried again to remember the poem.

It had moved and left no forwarding address.

So I gave the introduction a third time.

This time, where the poem should have been, the judges were treated to the spectacle of me running out of the room, disgusted with myself and humiliated.

I wasn't going to let this disaster just lie there. I knew I could be funny because I was always making my classmates laugh with my jokes and antics. I knew how to be the life of the party with my friends. So I came straight home and ran upstairs to my room. My mother asked me what I was doing and I said, "I'm going upstairs, I'm going to write something funny, and I'm going to go to the state championship!" So I went to my room and I wrote a piece called "Raisin Throwing: A Federal Offense" which involved me using sixteen different voices in eight minutes.

The next year, I went to the state championship in the "stand-up comedy" category.

After I unleashed the comic side of my personality, I led the pep rallies with Randy and landed the comic roles in the high school plays. I was voted class clown, but though I looked happy-go-lucky, I was struggling with serious issues on the inside. Making people laugh did nothing to fill my emptiness inside where I had a sincere craving for a reality beyond the superficial world of high school.

More and more, through high school, I began to experience a real hunger in my heart for something I could not identify. If you had asked me at the time, I suppose the best I could have done to put it into words was that I wanted "more." But it was not more material comfort. It was . . . something else. I couldn't put my finger on it. I can remember sitting at parties in my senior year at high school, watching people get drunk and passing around drugs. I didn't do drugs myself, but I remember thinking to myself in the middle of the haze and rock and roll, "There has to be more than this."

I began to search for answers in books. The titles of the books in my library began to change from *The Last of the Mohicans* to ones with a spiritual dimension. I read books on Eastern mysticism such as the *Tibetan Book of the Dead*, the *Bhagavad-gita*, and the ever-popular *Zen and the Art of Motorcycle Maintenance*. They all seemed to contain something just beyond my reach and none of them had anything to hold on to. Chanting and meditating did not bring me any answers, nor did books on "natural living" and "wilderness survival."

My room was filled with burning candles, in the hope that God would see how serious I was to know Him. Growing up Catholic, I didn't know how things worked, but I knew certain things. One thing I knew was: we burn candles (though I didn't know why). So I linked candle burning with spirituality. I had this notion that the mere burning of the candles would cause something to happen. (My parents feared I'd burn the house down, I had so many going.)

So now, as a freshman in college, the longing for something deeper with God, some more substantial contact with Him, had brought me to St. Hubert's again this evening.

In the pews down there, I had received the Eucharist every Sunday, but I did not know why. If I had been taught anything about it before my first Communion, I do not recall. I tried to pray, but didn't know what I was doing. And, at any rate, I wasn't sure if God was listening or interested in answering (if He was there at all). I thought about my religion classes I'd taken here at St. Hubert's, and tried to remember anything of importance that I might have learned from them. All I could really remember about it

was being dropped off, not wanting to go, and being resigned to it as I walked into the church with a sort of a
shrug. After that, it was primarily talk about feelings with
a mixture of those boring mid-'70s psycho-babble questions
that were all the rage then ("If you were a flavor of ice
cream, what flavor would you be? What's the weather in
your inner world like today? If you could write your own
creed what would it say?"). At best, this was to me like fla-
vorless chewing gum: 100% content-free. So, as I sat there
in the choir loft at St. Hubert's, I found that the only thing
I could remember from religion class was a cute blonde.

On the other hand, I could remember my preparation for
confirmation at St. Edward's when I was thirteen. I especially recalled the day I received the sacrament. As it is for
many young Catholics, confirmation was a blur of many
pictures, activities, and worries (such as "What if I'm called
on to answer questions by the bishop in front of God and
my friends?"). But out of the blur one thing stood out: a
gift my parents gave me of a black St. Joseph Edition Bible
with gilded pages and beautiful pictures. This gift seemed
like a great, mysterious treasure to me. I was excited at
the thought that this holy book, which I was accustomed
to seeing only in Mass, was now in my bedroom. I was
drawn to it as if it contained the secrets of the universe.
That night, I set it on my bed stand and determined that I
would read the whole thing through, one verse each night.
After about three weeks of that valiant attempt I gave up,
but I still held the Bible in great reverence. Maybe when
I was older I'd understand it, I thought. Soon after, the
Bible drifted over to my bookshelf.

And now, as I had done several times before, I was sitting
in the choir loft at St. Hubert's where the statues didn't
cry or twitch, feeling popular, funny, athletic, and com-

pletely empty and dead inside. Finally, after a few minutes
of waiting without result for I knew not what to happen,
I stood up and wandered out into the evening, alone and
lost. Inside, the sanctuary lamp kept burning.

Meeting the Love(s) of My Life

In September 1976, I enrolled at Normandale Junior College in Bloomington, Minnesota, to start on the core requirements for a degree in communications. I took a class called "Cultural Anthropology" during winter quarter. The very first day of classes, I walked in, sat down, opened my book, glanced up . . . and there was this beautiful girl with big brown eyes and lovely olive complexion. She entered the room and just radiated something so pure and so good. She had a peaceful countenance and a confident stride as though she wasn't looking for anything to add to her hidden treasure. She seemed different from the other girls I'd dated, and I immediately felt that I wanted to find out what she was like. Through the rest of class, and for days after, I couldn't take my mind off her. She'd walk into the class, and I'd just sit there and stare at her. I felt tongue-tied. It was weird. I didn't have a problem talking to anybody, but I had a problem approaching her. Finally, however, after a few days, I mustered the nerve to speak to her. I stood suavely outside the classroom with my arm leaning against the door so she had to notice me as she entered the room.

"Hi!" I said. It was an accomplishment.

She ducked beneath my arm to get through the door with barely a glance at me and a less than enthusiastic "hello."

I chose to believe she was interested.

The next day, in another attempt to impress her, I had my hair cut up to shoulder length and waited outside the door to say "Hi" again. At least this time she said "Hi" with a smile before walking past me.

"If it's the last thing I do, I'm going to go out with that girl," I whispered to one of my friends sitting next to me in class. I couldn't pay any attention to the teacher as I sat just staring at that sweet girl. She was petite, dark-haired, with eyes like a summer night, and her olive skin was so nicely tanned. I imagined her to be some exotic girl from the South Pacific straight out of a James Michener novel, which I was currently reading. I followed her to the student lounge, introduced myself, and asked her name.

"Emily," she said timidly. I sat down next to her and started to talk. She answered my questions about herself and I told her how I was editor of the school newspaper and a reporter for two local town papers. I didn't know what made her different, but I knew I wanted to get to know her better. What was the source of this inner beauty coming from her?

"What's your last name?" I asked.

"Tobler. It's Swiss, like Tobler chocolate," she explained. I wrote it down so I wouldn't forget. As soon as I was home, I thumbed through the phone book to find her number. Only three Toblers in the whole book. I called her that night to ask her out for bowling.

"Hi, Emily, this is Jeff."

After a pause she responded in a way no guy wants to hear, "Jeff who?"

"Remember? The guy who played goaltender in hockey?" I had mentioned this fact earlier that day. (Obviously I had made a big impression.) "Would you like to go out tonight?"

She said, "No."

I didn't know what to say after that, so I said, "Why not?"

She said, "Well, I have to babysit tonight."

I said, "I can wait until you're done babysitting. Then maybe we could go bowling or something."

She said, "Well, . . . then I have to, uh . . . wash my hair."

I said, "I can wait until you're done washing your hair."

She then came up with some other lame excuse but I wore her down until she finally said, "Well . . . I suppose."

Triumph! Late night bowling it was!

I had no idea that she was a teen leader at a Baptist youth group teaching "how not to go out with unbelievers."

In fact, I had no clue what sort of family I was walking into. All I knew was that I wanted to properly impress the Tobler family. So I donned my white bell bottoms, yellow silk shirt, and Elton John platform shoes. I ran a brush through my blonde David Cassidy hair and splashed on the Hai Karate before I left home in my dad's Fiat. I made sure to take along some photos of myself with the rock group "KISS," whom I had recently interviewed for the paper. Very impressive!

Yet for some reason, Mrs. Alice Tobler (a speaker for a full gospel, charismatic Christian group called "Women's Aglow") seemed less than thrilled to see my long-haired, white-bell-bottomed, platform-shoed self standing at her doorstep. She looked at me and allowed me one step into the house. I said, "While we are waiting for Emily, maybe you'd like to see some pictures of what I do?" There we were, all the members of "KISS" with blood all over their faces (it was part of the act), and me standing in the midst of them grinning.

She looked them over, nodded politely, excused herself, and headed up the stairs determined to tell her precious seventeen-year-old girl there was no way *this* hoodlum was going out with her.

But as she was halfway up the stairs, she said later, "The Lord just *stopped* me, spoke to my heart, and said, 'Let him go. He's going to preach the Gospel.'" She was astonished, but trusted God enough to let her only daughter go out with me.

So Emily came downstairs and we went out to my car. I was just ready to start the car when this diminutive, quiet, meek, five-foot, two-inch, 102-pound girl turns to me and says, "Do you know Jesus Christ as your personal Savior?"

I sat looking at the gas gauge with unusually focused vision. Somewhere in the distance, a dog barked. I thought, "What kind of night is this going to be?" I had never heard that before in my life. I had been praying hard in that choir loft at St. Hubert's and seeking God. I had driven many miles on my motorcycle with my helmet stuffed full of a thousand thoughts and questions. I had played those silly mind games where, if I saw four blue cars in the next mile, then Christianity was true, but if I saw four yellow cars then Buddhism was true. I had spent weeks, months, and years calling out to God to show Himself to me, but I had never heard that question before. So, when she said it, something hit me deep down inside.

But I didn't know what to say. So I said, "Yes. I'm Catholic!" But it was all bluff to cover my confusion. By it, I really meant (I suppose), "Ummm, I've heard of Jesus." For the reality was, I didn't know what she was talking about. The only other thing I could compare this to was a girl named Linda Christiansen who came up to me in the hall in high school once and said, "I belong to a prayer group here at school. We meet in the library. And I just wanted you to know we are all praying for you." I had said to her, "That's cool," but as she walked away, I felt anger well up inside of me. "She's really got it together," I thought to myself. I was jealous, wishing I had what she had. Like Emily, there had been something about her that was different.

My mind snapped back to the present. Emily was smiling as she asked another question more confusing than the first: "Do you speak in tongues?"

Interesting first date.

I didn't have a clue what she was talking about. I had never heard the biblical term from the book of Acts called "tongues," so naturally I replied, "Yeah. I speak in tongues." I looked carefully at her face to see if she was figuring me out. If she had, she didn't show it. She simply smiled at me, which I interpreted as, "She likes me!" Then she asked a few other questions, but I kept wondering what she was talking about. So, to strengthen my front, I wanted to ask her a question or two. However, I couldn't remember if she had said "tongues" or "lips." And so, in my effort to sound educated in the things of God, I casually turned to Emily and asked, "So, do *you* speak in lips?"

She burst into laughter, "It's tongues! Not lips!"

"Oh. That's what I meant, of course. What is 'tongues' again?"

"It's speaking in another language that God gives you in order to pray. If you want to know what it's about, I'll take you to this church called Jesus People Church so you can hear it if you'd like."

I was genuinely curious, but I knew my parents would not be at all enthused about me going to a non-Catholic church. At the bowling alley after a game or two we sat at a small table and talked. She asked me if I prayed often and I could honestly say "Yes" to that. I said the Our Father and the Hail Mary often. I told her I had been spending a lot of time praying and reading. I wanted her to tell me more, but I didn't want her to see me as the desperately hungry soul that I was. It was the most unusual date I had ever had. And I didn't even get a kiss!

After our first date, I started going over to her house and talking to her mother every day after school. Her mother could tell I was eager to learn about the Bible and spiritual things, so she would sit at that kitchen table and open up that blue Scofield Reference Bible and begin to talk to me about a personal relationship with Jesus Christ. I wanted to know what was so fascinating in that book that someone would wear it out. During that period, I couldn't stop thinking about the things she told me about Christ and about her relationship with Him. She told me about God's love for the world and how He offered salvation to everyone to bring them into a personal relationship with God. It wasn't just what she was saying, it was the way she was saying it. She had confidence, and I had never talked to anyone who spoke with confidence about their relationship with God. I wanted that.

One day, as we were reading, a passage of Scripture reached out and grabbed me. It was Galatians 2:20: "I have been crucified with Christ; it is no longer I who live, but Christ who lives in me; and the life I now live in the flesh I live by faith in the Son of God, who loved me and gave Himself for me." *Christ who lives in me*. Somehow, through this verse, it began to make sense to me that these people were different because of that. Christ was really living in them and animating their lives. No matter what they were talking about and no matter where they went, Christ was

a part of it. As each day passed, my desire to know Him
as they did gripped me as hunger grips a starving man.

At the same time this was going on, there was a sort of
lounge area at Normandale Junior College called the "Pit."
This was a place where all the Bible Christians gathered.
Between classes and on breaks, they would sit down there
and fellowship with one another. As my curiosity intensi-
fied, I started to hang around there and listen to them. I
was intrigued because they had this same sense of confidence that Emily exuded. So I introduced myself and then
quietly lurked around on the fringes of the conversation,
listening a lot and saying nothing (mostly because I didn't
know what to say). As the next few days passed, I started
attending classes less and less and hanging around the Pit
more and more. They talked the way Emily and her mom
did, full of love for God and confidence in their relationship
with Jesus Christ. What was more, I noticed that they had
Bibles similar to Mrs. Tobler's Bible: they were *worn* from
daily use and they *wrote* in them. I was very impressed.
These people were not all talk. They really knew God.
And for the first time, I began to wonder why nobody
I knew had ever talked to me about a personal relationship with Jesus Christ that I could remember. I thought,
"*This* is what I've been looking for: an intimate, personal
relationship with Jesus!" The enthusiasm the Toblers and
these people had for the Bible and for Jesus really made
me think.

Finally, on February 14, 1977, after about two weeks of
learning from Emily, her mother, and Christians at the
Pit about this relationship with Christ, I pulled over on
the side of the road in front of Flying Cloud Airport in
Eden Prairie, Minnesota, put my head down on the steer-
ing wheel of the car, and just began weeping. I cried out,

"Jesus, come into my heart! I want a new beginning! I want to be born again!"

And something happened. I felt as though all the anguish in me just drained away like water down the sink. I was filled to overflowing with a peace more profound than anything I had ever known. I sat there for about half an hour, in my car, crying and thanking God. This, I thought that evening, is what it is to be born again. I knew that something had happened to me that day and that I was changed. At long last, I felt, I had made contact with God. He had answered the prayer I had so fervently prayed a few months before in the balcony of St. Hubert's. And as I finally pulled myself together and pulled the car back onto the road, I had a profound sense at that moment that I would spend the rest of my life telling people about Jesus Christ.

When Worlds Collide

I sped home that night and walked into the house in a heavenly daze. I remember my mother looking at my flushed, tear-stained face and asking, "What happened to you?"

The only words I knew to describe my experience were the ones Emily and Mrs. Tobler had given me. "Mom!" I declared, "I've been *born again*!"

This term did not make my Catholic mother happy. "You *what*?" she said sharply.

"I got saved tonight!"

A shadow passed over my mom's face. She said in irritation, "Oh, Jeff. Don't you ever say that. You were a Christian the day you were baptized."

I said, "Mom, I don't know *what* happened the day I was baptized. But I do know what happened in my life tonight! I've given my life to Jesus! I've changed!"

Mom didn't want to hear any more about it. She had been concerned since I had become involved with a Protestant girl and her fears were confirmed with that statement. She frowned at me with a perplexed look on her face and left the room. Not long after, I went to bed more full of wonder and joy than I had ever been in my life and fell into a deep sleep.

My parents' sleep was fitful and troubled.

The next day I had one thing on my mind: getting a Bible. I had looked at the St. Joseph Edition Bible sitting on my bookshelf and decided it would not do. There were two reasons for this. First of all, it was huge and unwieldy,

more a family coffee-table Bible than one that you could
use on the road. But secondly, and perhaps more important, I wanted to buy a leather Bible like *Mrs. Tobler's and
the Christians at the Pit*. All I had to go by was copying
other people at this point since I didn't know what I was
doing or what "discipleship" meant. Neither Mrs. Tobler
nor the people at the Pit ever carried around their great
big family edition of the Bible. Rather, everybody had their
small portable Bible that they could write in and wear out.
So that was what I needed too, I decided. Therefore, I
grabbed my wallet, drove to Northwestern Bookstore in
Edina, Minnesota, marched in, and announced to the lady
at the counter, "Ma'am, I've been *born again!*"

She looked at me and said, "How nice."

I said, "I need to buy a Bible."

She said, "Here they are up here" and gestured to a huge
shelf filled with Bibles of all shapes and sizes. I didn't know
there were translations or anything. So I said, "I'd like the
brown one please. I'll get the brown leather one." It was
the same size as Mrs. Tobler's.

So she handed me the brown leather one, the New American Standard, a popular Protestant version. I paid for it,
walked out of the store, and went to our local priest.

"I've been *born again!*" I declared.

He looked at me the way the bookstore clerk had, and
said, "That's nice."

I said, "I bought this Bible. Would you bless it?"

He said, "Well, we don't normally do that."

I said, "Would you do it for me?"

He said, "All right," and he made the sign of the cross
over it and murmured a blessing.

"Can I make my confession?" I asked him. I hadn't gone
to confession in a very long time. We headed for the con-

fessional and I entered on the penitent's side. I opened the grate and began my confession.

The priest closed the grate.

I opened it.

He shut it.

"Can't I just talk to you? You know who I am!" I said in exasperation. He agreed and I finished my confession with the grate open.

As we emerged from the confessional, I asked him what book in the Bible I should read first.

"Why don't you start by reading the Gospels," he suggested.

"Which one?"

He said, "Read anything but John."

I said, "Why?"

He said, "It's very complicated and it might confuse you."

So I went home and read John.

I'm still not sure what my priest was worried about, because I was very blessed by John's Gospel and found it amazingly clear and understandable. In fact, John so whetted my appetite that I proceeded to devour the Bible. I couldn't put it down. In fact, when I arrived home with it, I took it upstairs, set it on my bed, and literally knelt down next to it, feeling like a famished man contemplating a porterhouse steak. Very gingerly, my hands went over the pages and I very carefully unstuck each page. There were two reasons for this. The first was that I really reverenced this book. The second was that I desperately did not want to look like a novice when I showed up at the Pit the next day. (It did not occur to my teenage brain that the shiny gold edges of the pages would give this away anyway.)

The next day, I went to Normandale and arrived in the Pit with my new Bible. And I felt like a kid with a new bat

at the ball field! I strode in with this confident swagger and
somebody asked me about my new Bible. I said casually,
"Oh yeah. This is my New American Standard version.
It's a fine translation." We chatted for a while and then I
skipped classes that day, spending the entire morning and
afternoon reading Scripture in the Pit — just like *they* did.
I watched carefully to see how they marked up their Bibles
with pens and highlighters because I wanted to do it right
and not permanently underline passages that weren't *really*
important. Soon, I got the hang of this and I really felt like
I belonged.

After this, I carried that Bible everywhere I went. I would
sit on the floor right outside the door of my classes, reading
it. I drove a motorcycle in those days and, not knowing
there were such things as Bible cases, I would wrap my
Bible up in a brown paper bag and then strap it to the
back of my bike with a bungee cord. Where I was, it was.

"Do you *have* to take that with you?" my mother would
ask in annoyance as we all piled into the car to head for
the store or anywhere else.

I couldn't help it. I felt so compelled to read it that I
not only took it with me everywhere, I skipped my college
classes and sat in the lounges reading it. I became a total
Bible fanatic. My family was embarrassed by this change
in me. From my perspective, I was thinking, "Hey! At
least I'm not drinking or getting in trouble as I had in the
past." But somehow they were more comfortable with the
Jeff they were used to, not this burgeoning Bible beater.

My best friend, Randy, felt much the same way. It was
kind of ironic really. In high school, we had spent many
hours sitting around his basement, drinking and talking
about "deep religious questions." But, of course, he had
never dreamed I would actually *do* something about all

that talk. So when I showed up at his door announcing I was born again and saved, he just thought I had gone off the deep end. As my commitment to Christ deepened, our friendship started to cool. He thought I was too much of a fanatic.

Around about this time, I developed the habit of going to the Perkins restaurant in Minnetonka, Minnesota, and sitting up all night long, drinking coffee and reading the Scriptures. If somebody would walk by, they would see the Bible and say, "Hmm, I see you have a Bible." Then I would say, "Yes! Sit down!" and I would tell everybody about what Jesus had done in my life and pray for people who needed prayer.

One particular evening, around midnight, I was sitting there reading my Bible and there was a group of girls at the table across from me. One of them kept looking at me, and when they rose to leave, she came over to me and said, "You're reading the Bible?"

I said, "Sure. Have a seat."

She sat down and the other girls left. I began to talk to her about my relationship with Christ and what had happened to me. I told her how I had given my life to the Lord and how He had changed me. As the conversation progressed, we began to talk about her life and she didn't tell me much about herself. But for some reason, I had this thought that kept coming to my mind: "The Lord knows about your abortion." At this point, I knew nothing about the charism or spiritual gift of knowledge. I just knew I was supposed to speak. So I blurted it out.

She broke down crying and said, "Only the doctor and I know about that. How did you know?"

I said, "I feel like the Lord has revealed this and that He wants you to know that He loves you."

We walked out of Perkins together and there in the parking lot we prayed together for her to receive Christ. Then I gave her my address and she left.

About two months later, I received a package in the mail. Inside, there was a little box with a Montana agate cross inside. Enclosed was a note from a jeweler saying, "I want to thank you so much for speaking to my daughter at Perkins a couple of months ago. I will probably never meet you, but I just want to thank you." It turned out that she was a runaway who had become involved in a very questionable life and, because of her conversion, her entire family had really come back together in a way that was centered around the Lord.

Seeing God move in such powerful ways built up my faith greatly. But I was still very naive, not to say gullible. I regarded everything from blowing of leaves to the patterns left by tires in the mud as a possible "sign" from God. I took it for granted that I might run into an angel around any corner. And so, I was a sitting duck when, one evening, a gentleman noticed me and my Bible, sat down beside me, and began to tell me all sorts of things from the book of Revelation that explained how the Pope was the antichrist. I had never heard such things before, but in my naiveté what he said seemed to make sense. He brought me out to his car and opened his trunk. Out dropped a huge chart, as if his trunk was a portable classroom. The chart graphed out the whole scenario from creation to the end of the world. I was astounded. In all seriousness, I looked around to make sure no one was listening and then leaned over to whisper to him in a confidential tone, "Tell me, are you an angel sent to tell me this message?" I was totally taken in by his information.

"Oh no," the gentleman laughed, "I am not an angel."

He gave me some literature and told me he'd like to keep in touch.

I zoomed home all excited to break this new information to my family. When I informed my mother that the Pope was the antichrist, she about went through the ceiling, but there was no arguing with me about Bible matters. I was the expert and she knew nothing. The next day I told Mrs. Tobler what I had learned from the gentleman at Perkins the other night.

"Oh Jeff. That man was a Jehovah's Witness. Don't listen to that sort of nonsense." She explained more about their beliefs and cautioned me not to accept just anything I came across that has to do with the Bible. This was a new wrinkle for me. I had just sort of assumed that the Bible was clear and that anybody quoting it couldn't possibly be speaking falsehood. Now Mrs. Tobler explained to me that it was very possible to take the Good Book and read it in a bad light. She explained that Jehovah's Witnesses do not believe in the divinity of Christ and showed the ways that they took Scripture out of context in order to make it appear to support their claims. She also showed that the things the man had said about the Pope being the antichrist were unfounded, slanderous, and unbiblical. She was not Catholic, but she had a sense of justice and fair play. By the time she was done, I felt a little foolish, and I regretted having fallen for what he said hook, line, and sinker. I did not, however, apologize to my mother for speaking evil of the Pope.

During that time, Emily took me to a church meeting held in a restored theater in downtown Minneapolis called Jesus People Church. She had explained to me it was a little unconventional. Sometimes people in the congregation would stand up and pray out loud. The church was made up of mostly ex-hippie Jesus freaks and charismatics of all kinds. I looked around at all the smiling faces and people holding their fat Bibles. The musicians played guitars and drums and several lively singers swayed back and forth on the stage. Suddenly, a man behind me burst out in a deep voice saying something I couldn't understand.

"What's that?" I gasped.

"That's tongues!" Emily whispered loudly through her smile.

"Oh!" I said, realizing now what she had meant on our first date. After he stopped, a woman on the other side of the auditorium stood up and shouted in English.

"What's that?" I asked, feeling the hair stand up on the back of my neck.

"That's the interpretation."

"Oh," I said, not understanding what was going on. I began to feel very nervous. *What if they call on me to pray?*

It was the old fear of public speaking rearing its head. And not without some cause. Once, not long after my discovery of Jesus, I had gone to a small church and somehow wound up with a group of elders praying before the service. Suddenly, one of the elders had turned to me and said the most terrifying thing I could have imagined: "I feel as though the Lord is saying that you have a word to give to us."

I looked around the circle like a deer caught in the headlights. I wondered what on earth the "word" I was supposed to give might be. Cucumber? Squid? *What* word? I literally thought he meant a single word and I had no idea what to do. Finally, I said, "I don't think I have any word." The man replied, "I've been listening to the Lord for a long time and I think I know when the Spirit is telling me you have a word. So just speak right out."

I swallowed hard and tried to think. Finally, I looked at him, and said, "What would you like me to say?"

At this point, Emily (bless her heart) intervened and explained how truly clueless I was. So they let the matter drop. But it was a close call.

So, with that kind of experience under my belt, there I sat in Emily's church, bracing myself just in case somebody asked me to pray or something. If they did, I had written a prayer and tucked it under the band of my watch. It began with the "Hail Mary." Talk about worlds in collision!

And it really was two worlds for me. Because all this time, while I was increasingly bopping around town to these various Pentecostal and Assembly of God-type church meetings, I was still going to the Catholic Church with my parents. Eventually, I found out there was a Catholic charismatic prayer group in my parish. They listened to audiotapes of Fr. John Bertolucci and Fr. Mike Scanlan. So I went there for a while. Partly I did it because I was trying to reconcile these two worlds and partly I did it because I needed ammunition in the growing conflict with my parents. Whenever they questioned me about my attendance at Pentecostal prayer meetings, I could brandish Fathers Scanlan and Bertolucci at them and say, "See! *They're* normal! *They're* Catholic! And *they're* all excited about the Lord!"

But the conflict was growing between my parents and me anyway. And a huge part of it was my fault. For as time went on, life at home was becoming less and less about me speaking of Jesus in love and more and more about me finding any and every argument with which to defeat my parents, denigrate their Faith, and constantly compare it unfavorably to mine. Much of this was, of course, very subtle — like spiritual guerrilla warfare. I would leave my

Bible out in prominent locations "in order to witness to
them." I would compare the "dead faith" of Catholics to
the excitement of the true spirituality that *I* knew so deeply.
I would speak dismissively of their apparently lifeless lack
of relationship with God. I became increasingly insuffer-
able. Worse still, as the deep tension between my parents
and me grew it filled our house. My two younger sisters,
Jayne and Leslie, felt it too. But nothing could be said that
would change my mind. I was getting pretty offensive with
my in-your-face "I'm right. You're wrong. You're going to
Hell. You need what I have" type of Christianity.

On the other hand, there was real sincerity there too. For
all my cockiness, I genuinely grew in my desire to preach
or teach the Bible for the rest of my life. Up until now, I
had considered acting or broadcasting, but I was becoming
increasingly gung-ho to be a Minister of the Word. Yet I
was still going to the Catholic Church and trying to work
it out. In a funny way, none of my problems with the Catholic Church were theological or doctrinal at this stage. It
was all experiential. All I knew was that Jesus had come
into my life in a new way and I wanted to spend the rest
of my life sharing that Life. When I looked at Catholics in
the parish I did not see this excitement. It was this contrast,
not any doctrinal consideration, that motivated my growing hostility toward the Catholic Church. I just wanted to
know Jesus better and Preach the Word. What that would
mean for my life I did not yet know.

Love and Anguish

The bite of winter had turned to springtime, and I would often take off on my motorcycle and think. I had developed such a love for Scripture that the pages of *my* Bible were now worn. And I was filled with the desire, not only to learn it, but to teach it too. After a lot of thinking, I was getting serious about going to a place called Christ for the Nations Institute in Dallas, Texas.

My parents weren't too happy about this since CFNI was a Protestant Bible school. In fact, it came to the point where my dad would say, "I don't want to hear any more about Jesus, the way you are talking about Him. How are you going to pay for Bible college? What good will it do you? Can you get a job teaching the Bible? You have scholarships from other schools for acting. Jeff, you're not thinking straight." (It is not common to hear parents complain to their kid, "Why can't you do the sensible thing and pursue *acting?*") But my mind was made up. I was crazy about the Bible and that's what I wanted to do.

Besides, not only was I crazy about the Bible, I was crazy about Emily. I thought, "Boy, it would be really nice to marry someone like this. Someone who is on fire for the Lord."

Not coincidentally, Emily was also planning to go to Christ for the Nations Institute with her best friend, Jeannie, and a close friend of hers named Dan, whom she had known since she was a child. Many had assumed Emily and Dan would get married because of their close relationship. Dan had already attended one year of Bible school and soon he would be back in Minnesota for the summer. As you might guess, I was not without my feelings of jealousy toward Dan, but I intended to act like a gentleman when he arrived. It had been rumored that Dan had visited Emily earlier in the year with presents and the intention to propose, but had never asked due to Emily's hesitancy about marrying so young. That was encouraging. And my spirits were further buoyed when I received word from Emily in late spring that he was engaged to a girl at Christ for the Nations Institute.

I thought, "Yes!" The door to a future with Emily seemed to be opening wider, even though she didn't give *me* much evidence to go on. When I would visit Mrs. Tobler, she would encourage me to hang in there.

On a very strange summer evening, Emily, Jeannie, Dan, and his fiancée, Connie, and I met at the Chalet pizza parlor in Chanhassen (just across the street from St. Hubert's) to discuss plans of driving to Dallas for Bible school. They had persuaded me to go along with them, but I was really torn. If Emily wasn't serious about me, then what would I be getting myself into?

I was making conversation, and I began to say, "When I finish Bible college, I'm going to do thus and so . . ." Suddenly, Emily gave me a look of utter surprise and said, "How can you do that if we're married?"

Time stood still.

I said, "Come again?" All conversation at the table ceased.

She repeated herself.

I stammered, "Could we . . . could we talk outside for a moment?"

We went outside. "What is going on?" I said with rising hope. "Did you say, 'married'?"

"Yes, I thought you wanted to marry me," she said with her face upturned toward mine.

"Yes, yes, I do!" I said before she could change her mind. "What made you decide that we should?"

"I realize how serious you are to learn the Bible and know God. I always wanted to marry someone who loved God more than he loved me. You seem to be the right one for me."

It wasn't exactly what I hoped she'd say. (I'd hoped for something like, "I think you're the most wonderful, handsome, intelligent man in the world and I'm madly in love with you!") But I took her offer and said, "Great!"

I thought, "Hey! I just went out for pizza!" This was turning out to be one of my better days.

However, being romantics at heart, we did not formalize our engagement then and there. Instead, a few days later, on June 24, 1977, I took Emily to Lake Harriet in Minneapolis, Minnesota. We walked through the Rose Garden and sat down on a bench overlooking the lake. There, in a much more suitable setting than a pizza parlor parking lot, I proposed to her and to my joy and wonder, she said, "Yes!" Soon after, we went to her grandmother's house on the banks of the Rum River in Milaca, Minnesota, and I asked Emily's father, Andreas, for her hand. After, we waded out into the river a bit and when we were knee-deep, I produced an engagement ring and slipped it on her finger.

So it was decided that Emily and I would go down to Dallas and go to school. By this time, I had graduated from drinking coffee and reading Scripture all night at Perkins to actually waiting tables there. So I worked like a madman all summer to pay off the diamond engagement ring I bought her.

Meanwhile, the ripples from my conversion and engagement continued to spread. All through high school, I had dated a girl named Karen and we had broken up as I entered college. One day in the summer of '77, I was driving somewhere and noticed a car broken down on the side of the road with a woman standing and looking perplexed. So I pulled over to help. Who should it turn out to be but Karen? I offered her a ride and she accepted. But she was mighty quiet.

So to break the ice I said, "How are you doing?"

She said, "Fine."

I said, "Have you heard what happened to me?"

She said, "*Oh* yeah" with a lift of the eyebrows and a straight-ahead stare.

I said, "Whaddaya think?"

She said, "You're nuts."

Happily, right about then the gas station came into view and I dropped her off.

Karen's feelings more or less mirrored those of my parents by this time. I was nineteen years old and Emily was eighteen. They were pleased that I was getting married, and they liked Emily a great deal. But they were increasingly worried that I was simply being reckless and irresponsible. They would ask questions like, "How are you going to support yourself? You're going to have a *wife*, for Heaven's sake!"

"God'll provide!" I would reply with that big smug smile. Their exasperation grew. It was one thing to throw myself into some cockamamie adventure. It was another thing to

drag Emily along with me into poverty and religious ma-
nia. But the more they tried to get me to listen to reason,
the more infuriatingly and cheerfully dismissive of their
concerns I was. In both words and attitude, I made it clear
that I was being truly spiritual and my mind was on the
things of the kingdom of Heaven while they were being
worldly, crass, materialistic, and, in essence, faithless. They
needed to become real Christians — like me. After not too
much of this know-it-all treatment from me, it came to
the point where all I had to do was mention Jesus and my
father would look up at me from under his eyebrows and
dart me a glance that said very clearly, "Jeff . . . don't . . .
go . . . there." Meanwhile, my mother knew that I was
an impulsive person and assumed that this phase also was
going to pass. So she tried to argue with me that it was a
mistake to go to Christ for the Nations Institute because
I would leap in with both feet and then get bored with it
in a few months and bail. I was, they said with increasing
passion, making *major* life decisions about school, work,
and marriage without sufficient care and planning. To me,
this was just further evidence that the Catholic Church
was hardening people's hearts against God and cooling the
flames of the love of Christ.

Finally, on a hot night in August — the night before I
left for Bible school — I was standing up in my bedroom
and my dad came up to talk to me. My dad was by now
deeply frustrated with me.

"How are you going to support a wife?" my father asked.
I tried, once again, to wave it all away lightly, but he pressed
me. "You don't have a job or any skills to make a living.
Why do you have to go to Dallas? There are hardly any
Catholics down there. Use your *head*, Jeff. How are you

going to pay for school?" He had brought these issues up to me many times, but I would not listen now any more than I had before.

"God will provide," I said with blithe confidence (truth to tell, I really had no idea how we would make it financially).

As the conversation progressed, my dad and I got into a hotter and hotter argument. All the anger and frustration over my self-righteous behavior came boiling out of my father.

"You're always drawing distinctions between the churches you go to and our church," he said in frustration.

I said, "Well, when I go to those other churches, the people there all have their own Bibles! How come we don't bring our Bibles to church? What are we? Afraid of Scripture? Why don't Catholics read their Bibles?"

My father sighed in annoyance. He didn't know what to say, so, of course, he said, "Jeff, you don't understand . . ."

I cut him off. "These other people share their faith. How come we don't talk about it? What are we ashamed of? What are you and Mom ashamed of?"

My dad's face was beginning to get flush, but I just went on delivering body blows.

"The Christians I know pray for the sick. Why don't we pray for the sick? Why is it, when we go to Mass, even healthy people look pretty sick and sad themselves? The Christians I know are happy! They're filled with the joy of the Lord. But us? We're so dead! Why is our faith so dead? It feels like a funeral every time we go to Mass!"

My father was struggling to master his mounting anger but by now I was only interested in one thing: defeating him. So as he tried to govern his frustration at my abuse of his Church and articulate some sort of reply, I ignored him. Instead of listening, I zeroed in for the kill and began to dredge up any and every ugly little news item I had heard recently about priests who had fallen into sexual or financial sins of one kind or another. I also made sure to add that at Jesus People Church, a lot of the people there were people who had been raised Catholic until "their eyes had been opened." It was hateful and it was calculated to hurt him.

It did. All at once, my insolence was just too much for my father and in a last attempt to knock some sense into me, he struck me — for the first time ever — across the cheek. He knocked me clear off my feet and I landed in my closet. I screamed something out in anger after him as he left the room. I could not understand why my family was not happy for me or excited about the path I had chosen. I began to sob. This wasn't the way I had expected to leave home.

I thought, "I can't figure this out! I'm not partying, I'm not drinking, I'm not messing around or anything! I've given my life to Jesus and I can't understand this response from my family!" I was genuinely confused. From the moment I had come home to announce my commitment to Jesus until now I had received from my parents the one response I never expected. Just where I thought my parents would be the most proud of me, I was instead finding the biggest obstacle I had ever faced. I genuinely and desperately wanted to be pleasing to my parents. In its own weird way, even all my holier-than-thou rhetoric was an attempt to wring their approval out of them by beating them in arguments. What better thing, I wondered, could parents ask for than a son who comes home and says, "I'm not going to drink anymore. I'm not smoking or partying anymore. I'm going to live a holy life." And now here I was, alone, my cheek smarting from the only blow I had ever received from my father's hand. What was wrong with them? I couldn't figure it out.

The next day, Emily and her friends picked me up and I left home. Just as I left, Dad handed me an envelope containing $800. I wanted to say, "See! God provided!" but I had enough sense not to.

I can remember looking back and seeing my father and mother in the driveway as we drove off down the street. I drove away with Emily without apologizing or making any attempt at amends with my family. It was in this way and in this spirit that I left home for Bible school — to become a pastor.

Adventures in Bible School

The year at Christ for the Nations Institute was a big adjustment for me. I was in a totally non-Catholic environment and very soon I was attending the Sunday worship meeting on campus rather than going to Mass. It never occurred to me that there might be a problem with this. I still considered myself Catholic, but my main interest was simply in learning about Scripture and in praising Jesus wherever a bunch of Christians happened to get together to do so. At Christ for the Nations Institute, they did so on Sunday mornings, so I did too. Curiously though, it never seemed to me that I had actually been to church without having received the Eucharist. I had the dim, inarticulate sense that we were missing something important that was there in my old Catholic parish. I was still more Catholic than I liked to let on.

On the other hand, when I went to Mass, I constantly fell into the trap of spending the entire Mass looking around at the quiet (at the time I said "dead") people in the pews next to me and making constant comparisons between them and the "on fire" Pentecostal worship services. I was judge, jury, and executioner of all the other parishioners at the Catholic church I attended (when visiting my family, never in Dallas). I would sit there throughout the Mass, thinking to myself, "Just look at these people! These ignorant, dumb Catholics. They don't know Christ, they don't know the Word of God, *they don't even know what they're doing here*! What a waste of time!" I would sit there thinking,

"I wish I could — just once — get up in that pulpit for just fifteen minutes and let people know what Christ is all about." It frustrated me deeply that so many Catholics — like my father and mother — simply couldn't comprehend what I had come to see so clearly. On the other hand, I sometimes found myself quite torn, particularly when fellow students would attack the Catholic Church. At such moments, something inside of me would rear up in defense of the Church, even though I had no particular intention of making it part of my life. It was kind of like defending the sibling you don't get along with: yes, he's a nuisance, but don't insult my brother. (As far as I was concerned, the church you went to wasn't the issue. It was *Jesus* who was the issue. So I was as opposed to those who said you *can't* be Catholic as I was to those who said you should be. I called this state of confused inner conflict "being balanced.")

Academically, I learned a tremendous amount about the Bible at Christ for the Nations Institute and I worked very hard. School began with morning prayer. I would spend time in prayer with God in the chapel. Then there would typically be three or four classes during the day (studying the Old and New Testaments, exegesis, hermeneutics, pneumatology, etc.). Classes were big and exciting. Oftentimes, teachers would, right in the middle of class, break into praise and prayer and we students would join in. Sometimes the teacher would change the direction of the conversation right in the middle of class in response to what he believed to be the prompting of the Holy Spirit. As a student, that really kept me on my toes.

In addition, we had some of the best known speakers in charismatic and Assembly of God circles come through the school on a weekly basis. These people (such as Kenneth Copland, Marilyn Hickey, Larry Lea, Derek Prince,

Cookie Rodriguez, and Kenneth Hagin), though not terribly well known in Catholic circles, were big names in that sector of Christendom. It made us feel like kids in a candy shop. As a result, we were exposed to ministry after ministry after ministry of people who were going out into the world and making a difference in evangelism (provided they were Pentecostal. We regarded Lutherans, Methodists, and other mainline Protestant groups as being in just as much need of salvation as Catholics).

Not only were the speakers from all over the place, the students were from all over the world as well. My roommate was from Guyana in South America. He was considered the smartest guy on campus (and would later go on to start a Bible college in Trinidad). His name was Charles Ceres. My other roommate, Brad Cooper, was from Iowa. And we all came together in the full expectation that the Holy Spirit was still manifesting His gifts in and through Christians today.

And we had good reason for thinking so. Charles was fluent in other languages. One morning when I woke up, Charles looked at me and said, "Jeff! The most extraordinary thing happened last night!"

I said, "What?"

He said, "You sat up on your bed and you began to speak French!"

I said, "I don't know any French."

He said, "You were giving me directions from the Lord for my life!"

I snorted, "Naaaaah! Come on."

He said, "Yes, Jeff. It's true!"

I looked at him and he was serious as a heart attack. Everyone regarded him not only as the brightest but as one of the most honest and truthful people on campus. He had incredible integrity. And he wasn't blinking or suppressing a smile or given to flights of hysteria. He was on the level.

So finally I said, "If this ever happens again, wake up Brad. I'd kinda like to verify it."

The very next night, it happened again. I just sat up and started talking to him in my sleep — in French. So Charles woke Brad up and said, "Brad! Brad! Listen! Listen!" Brad listened in amazement and the next day he told me, "Sure enough! You sat up and you were talking to him in fluent French."

I'm still unsure what to make of this incident. It has only happened to me one other time in my life. That was before a prayer meeting several years later. As we prayed, I began praying in tongues, and the guest speaker, who was from Poland, said, "I didn't realize you knew Polish." I said, "I don't know a lick of Polish." He said, "You were praising God in complete, fluent Polish." Praise God for His odd and wonderful marvels!

Such displays of the Holy Spirit's power did not go unchallenged by the evil one. Where God is active, Satan is always busy trying to oppose Him. There was no exception in this case. Christ for the Nations Institute was located in a particularly seedy and dangerous area near Dallas called Oak Cliff. It was the roughest suburb of Dallas. We were warned before we went there that it could be unsafe at times and that we needed to watch ourselves. On the first day of Bible college, I checked in and then headed over to Mary Martha Hall to help Emily get her things moved in. (The school did not permit men to go into the female students' rooms, but I could help bring things into the building.) Just as we were getting started, a helicopter flew over and a loud voice came booming out of its speaker system:

"GET IN YOUR ROOMS! GET IN YOUR ROOMS!"
We all looked around, bewildered.

"What is this?" somebody asked.

There was no time to talk. The residential assistants bustled us all into the building double time and before I knew it, we were suddenly in the women's dorm, stuffed under beds, with women looking at us. I was thinking, "Hello! Welcome to school!"

When the dust settled and they let us come out from under the beds, we found out that there had been some lunatic running around campus with a sawed-off shotgun.

That was my first day of Bible college.

And that was nothing compared to the day I was shot in the head.

It happened this way. For a brief period, I held two jobs. Emily and I worked at a hotel called the DuPont Plaza, where we were waitress and waiter. Afterward, I zoomed over to a Mobil station near campus to work my second job. One evening, I was in transit to my second job, cruising down the road on my motorcycle followed by Emily and a friend in her friend's car. Suddenly, a pickup truck pulled up next to me and the driver rolled down his window. I looked over and to my astonishment the passenger reached across the driver's chest with a pistol and fired at me.

The bullet struck the top of my helmet and ricocheted off. In terror, I slammed my face down on the bike, gunned it, and took off as fast as I could go. Behind me, I heard a rapid series of gunshots — Pop! Pop! Pop! — as the truck receded in the distance. (Emily, all the while, was thinking the truck was backfiring or something.)

I drove like a maniac just to get as far away from that truck as I could. Finally, I reached the Mobil station and pulled in. I couldn't even speak, I was in such shock. We called the police and they took down all the information. However, I don't know if they ever caught the guys. Interestingly, this was the one and only night in all of Bible college when my dad called me. It was a real comfort to hear his voice, though I was too shaken to say more than a few words.

During this same period of time there had been a string of service station robberies in the vicinity. The thief's *modus operandi* was frighteningly consistent. The gas station attendant was forced to lay face down with his hands behind his back and then he was shot in the back of the head. I decided I'd been shot in the head enough and so quit my job at the Mobil station soon after this. The week after I quit, the station was held up and the attendant (another student at Christ for the Nations Institute) was forced to lay on his face with his hands behind his back — and, strangely and miraculously, he was spared. The robbers got away with the money, but he was not murdered, thanks be to God.

Another time, Emily and I found jobs at the local International House of Pancakes. It was at IHOP that I began to learn one of the deep truths about spiritual warfare. It wasn't just going on "out there" in the neighborhood. It was going on inside of me as well. It happened this way.

One day, I was on shift as a cook while Emily was waitressing. For several days, I had been telling one of the other cooks — a drug dealer named Little Man — about Jesus and how he needed to be born again. Little Man, for his part, was doing his best to sneer and ridicule everything I said. The harder I tried, the more difficult he tried to make things. One night Little Man was taunting me during a busy rush and the ticket wheel was filled with orders. He refused to help me. He stood at the far end of the kitchen with his arms folded, mocking me.

"I'll give you ten seconds to get over here and start cooking," I said evenly. I could feel my hand start to tremble.

"Let's see you cook, white boy!" he laughed.

I put down my spatula and lunged for him, grabbing him around the neck. I lifted him up and rammed him against the cooler and continued to choke him. A swarm of waitresses including Emily raced back and tried to pull me off of him. Finally I let him drop. Little Man gasped for air and then scrambled to his feet to grab a huge butcher knife. As he moved to come after me, one waitress who knew Little Man well, kicked the knife from his hand just like in the movies. He left, but not before threatening to return with a gun.

I couldn't believe what I had done. What a way to show someone the love of Jesus! And what a stupid thing for me to do! It was *not* a good idea to make enemies in a neighborhood like Oak Cliff. I think it was God's protection that kept Little Man from shooting me later that night. I did apologize to him and things worked out between us, but I was disturbed over the frightening anger that had gripped me.

So was Emily. One day, during our time at CFNI, as we were getting on my motorcycle, Emily and I were arguing about something insignificant and I became so angry I picked up my motorcycle and threw it. I always took great care of my bikes and I couldn't believe what I had done and that I had the strength to actually lift it. Emily was so frightened of me, she backed away and cried, "Don't kill me!"

That brought me to my senses. I apologized for my behavior and told her I would never hurt her. "I have to get some help for my anger. I don't want to behave this way." We talked for a while and decided that I should visit one of the school counselors, which I did. The man, Carroll Thompson, prayed over me and I felt a heavy weight lift away from me. From that day on, my temper began to abate and though I could still experience passionate anger, it never displayed itself with that kind of physical violence again. There was a marked change and I was taking my first steps on the road to healing.

Finally, the year of Bible school ended and it was time to head back to Minnesota for our wedding. My parents had insisted that we get married in the Catholic Church so, to keep the peace, we agreed. We did not have a Mass at the wedding, however. We invited the minister from the Tobler's Methodist church to co-officiate the ceremony. It was a tense arrangement between a staunch Catholic family and a devout Protestant one. Curiously, Emily and I never discussed what church we would be a part of. She assumed we would be Protestant, but at the time I had no focused intention of leaving the Catholic Church completely. As for Emily, she knew little about the Catholic Church. She was not anti-Catholic, she was just unaware of Catholic doctrine. In fact, I was the first Catholic person she had ever really known. Everything was still about Jesus as far as I was concerned and I still was not thinking in terms of any particular church or denomination at all. Questions about denominations weren't even on the map for me. On the other hand, though I was not *thinking* in my mind about leaving the Church, I believe it is accurate to say I had already emotionally (in my gut) done so.

We attended the pre-marriage classes (something about

"compatibility tests") but, as far as I can recall, the priest never explained to us about the importance of the sacrament of marriage, the ramifications of a mixed marriage, or any of the doctrinal teaching of the Church on marriage. He did ask us if we were willing to raise any children we might have as Catholics, a question we found difficult to answer. From our perspective we were compatible and ready for marriage and so, in a lovely ceremony on June 3, 1978, Emily and I were wed in St. Hubert's Catholic Church in Chanhassen, Minnesota.

Like all newlyweds, we had no idea what the future held.

Leaving the Church

After one year of Bible school, and now newly wed, I began to feel that thing called "reality" exerting pressure on me. Just how *was* I going to support my wife? Finally, I decided to move back to Minneapolis and go to radio and television broadcasting school. I did so, and while in school I landed a job at WCCO radio in Minneapolis. The great part about this job was that it entailed me escorting all sorts of celebrities around town as guests of the station (which meant I was able to witness to all sorts of people). I remember spending one whole day with Sophia Loren: just Sophia Loren and me talking about Jesus all day. Though I was in great awe of her, I felt compelled to speak to her about Jesus because I knew she was Roman Catholic. I had a strongly-held conviction that Catholics didn't have a personal relationship with God and I figured she needed to know. She conveyed to me that her Catholic Faith meant a great deal to her and was very satisfying and meaningful. She also spoke with great passion about her love for her husband and children. At the end of the day, Sophia agreed to have her bodyguard take a picture of her planting a big smooch on my cheek. The bodyguard, it turned out, was a better bodyguard than photographer, however. So to this day our family photo album has a picture of the bodyguard's thumb in front of the camera lens, obscuring the Sophia Smooch.

Other guests were not quite so amiable. Once I witnessed

to Bella Abzug. It didn't go over well. I chauffeured Walter Cronkite around town and told him about Jesus. Another time, I witnessed to the late Madalyn Murray O'Hair, founder of American Atheists, and I was almost fired for doing so.

Perhaps the oddest story during this time was the day I was supposed to meet Leonard Nimoy and ferry him someplace or another. We were supposed to meet on Second Avenue in downtown Minneapolis. I was waiting for his limo to arrive when I realized I had to use the restroom. So I went in the building.

As I entered the restroom, I glanced at the other guy in there.

It was Leonard Nimoy.

Without even thinking, I stuck out my hand to shake his hand and exclaimed, "Spock!"

"Leonard Nimoy," growled the author of *I Am Not Spock*.

I burbled, "Oh! I'm sorry! *Leonard Nimoy*!" I continued shaking his hand enthusiastically and chattering. I'm not sure what he made of it, but the whole moment made an indelible impression on *my* memory. After all, I was still basically just a kid barely out of my teens.

But though I was young, I was eager to learn and my employers seemed to have a lot of confidence in me. And a result was that I not only was able to meet a lot of interesting people, I also was able to do a lot of interesting things. WCCO was a perennial winner of the Peabody Award (a prestigious award for excellence in broadcasting) and had a very high reputation for quality. It is one of the largest stations in the country. But while I was there, they went on strike and I suddenly found myself as the only one at the station with a first-class broadcasting license. So I received a call at midnight from Phil Lewis, the general manager, telling me, "You've gotta come in to run the station!"

Suddenly, this fantasy I had entertained in the back of my mind for years of being in broadcasting and *specifically* of doing it at WCCO fell out of the sky and into my lap. Out of the blue, I found myself being told, in a midnight phone call, "You are running the entire operation!" That meant I was doing not only engineering, but I was on the air for two weeks, holding the whole thing together with chewing gum and chicken wire. So there I was, this twenty-year-old kid running Peabody Award-winning WCCO, subbing for Boone and Ericsson, Steve Cannon, *Hobbs House*, and all these other shows that were the staple of our daily fare. It was wild. Talk about baptism by fire!

After I graduated from broadcasting school, we went to Valley City, North Dakota. My reputation as a fanatical Christian had reached the staff of KOVC (the station where I was hired) and they were on guard for any attempts at quoting the Bible to them. They even took bets on how long it would take before I tried to convert one of them. I did approach one of the announcers, Larry, not long after I started working there. He said to me, "If you want to talk to me about Jesus, you'll have to come to the bar, because that's where I'm headed."

I took him up on his offer and we spent several hours together while I shared with him how Jesus could change his life. He was struggling with personal problems. That night he made a decision to follow Jesus. After he went home, he shared the change with his wife and she too turned her life over to Jesus. They became involved in a local church and spent hours studying their Bibles. They have remained friends with us over the years and it has been great to see them raise their children to love God.

Larry later worked for a Christian broadcasting network for many years.

Many teenagers came to the radio station to watch the DJs. I invited them into the studio on the condition that they would let me tell them about Jesus. Several did come in and learned about how much Jesus loved them. They repented of living in sin and began to share Jesus with other teens in the high school. It was exciting to see the revival among the young people in this small town.

I also discovered a convent with several charismatic nuns just outside of town. I went to the convent each morning and prayed with the sisters and puttered around in the garden with them. We quickly became close and they became a source of uplifting fellowship to me. One evening, I invited them to come down to the radio station while I was on the air. It was late in the evening and I was in the studio with five of the nuns in full habit, listening to popular Christian music. I turned down the rock 'n' roll that was broadcasting over the radio so we could hear the Christian music in the studio. One particular song was very lively and all of us began to dance to the music. Our lively praise was interrupted when we looked up and saw the general manager standing at the front door looking into the studio. He walked to his office and shut the door while I shooed the nuns out the back door and turned off the music. I wondered what was going to happen now.

The next morning, the general manager called me into his office. I sat in front of his desk nervously. He did not look up at me as he began, "I run a radio station. Last night," he paused, "I came into that radio station and I saw one of my announcers dancing with five nuns." He let a long pause elapse. "It will never happen again, will it?"

"No sir!" I replied.

"Now get back to work," he said, still not looking up.

"Yes sir," I said, hurrying from his office, thankful I still had my job.

Now all this time I still had never quite quit the Catholic Church. In fact, it became my habit (pardon the pun) to go to the convent outside town every morning. Along with the nuns, I would go to Mass in the morning real early, and then on Wednesday and Sunday, I would go to the Assembly of God church to hear preaching on the Bible. I was still working in radio, but I had this abiding hunger inside to preach the gospel.

I began to explore the opportunities within the Catholic Church at the time and found them to be very slim for a young married man. I would have to wait until I was 35 to become a deacon, and that seemed like an eternity to wait for a young man of twenty-one. At that time, 1980, lay people did not play such a vibrant role in the Church leadership as is common in many parishes today. In my frustration, I looked elsewhere for a place to serve.

The small, local Assembly of God church had a young pastor named Pete Weisenberger. He and his wife became our friends. After we had attended the Wednesday night Bible studies for some time, they asked me to teach. I was eager to do so. After several months, the Assembly of God pastor, knowing my deep desire to preach and teach the gospel, offered to have me become Pastor of Evangelism for that church. It would entail visiting prisons, nursing homes, and state hospitals, as well as general preaching and teaching. I dove into this work with zest. At last, it seemed as though I was finding a place where I could make a difference for God.

But at the same time, my heart was increasing in anger and coldness toward the Catholic Church. Three major things in particular happened during this period that formed three different focal points for my growing bitterness.

First, I went over to study Scripture with a local priest. I was looking for a way to foster fellowship in the Catholic Church as well as to cultivate my love of Bible study in a Catholic setting. But as we got together to study, I was faced with a disappointment that seemed to sum up so much of my experience with Catholics. We sat down together, the priest and I, and I said, "Let's turn to the book of Hebrews." (I had a question I wanted to ask about.)

The priest fumbled about in his Bible for a minute and then asked *me* for help. He didn't know where the book of Hebrews was in the Bible.

I was embarrassed for him and I was angry for myself. I thought to myself, "What am I going to learn here when I know more than the priest does?" I felt deflated. Soon after, we stopped meeting.

Another deep discouragement came in the form of another priest who periodically popped in to do some sort of "Word of Inspiration" show at the station I worked at. Father was habitually nervous going on the air and carried a small bottle of whiskey in his pocket from which he would take a drink before the broadcast to settle his nerves. I was completely scandalized by this, particularly because the environment at Christ for the Nations had strongly socialized me to regard any alcohol consumption as sinister.

Finally, I became really angry at my local parish. It was like this. As a radio DJ, I received lots of opportunities to witness to kids who came by the station. Every kid wants to see the rock 'n' roll DJ, so I would invite local kids down to the station, but, again, their ticket into the place consisted of their being willing to listen to a reading from

Scripture. So we would sit there in the broadcast booth and I would turn the music down and give them a short Bible lesson. In this way, I led dozens of kids (including the Homecoming King and Queen) to Jesus Christ.

So there was a little rock and roll DJ revival going on in the local high school age group with a couple dozen kids all on fire for Jesus. Now some of these kids went to the Catholic high school. I hoped the Catholic high school environment would help to support these kids in their newfound commitment to Christ. However, to my shock, I went with the nuns one night to a dance up at the Catholic school and walked into a deafening scene which featured recordings of a heavy rock group singing about such noble Christian activities as having sex in the back seat of a car and so forth. I sat there in astonishment and watched not just clueless students, but seemingly clueless Catholic parents and teachers dancing to these hymns of lust without batting an eye. I couldn't figure this out. After being to Bible school and being around Evangelicals and Fundamentalists, I could not fathom how Catholics could allow this type of thing to happen in the Church. How *could* we put up with music that was basically mind pollution and opposed to everything Christ stood for? For the first time, I consciously said to myself, "I don't belong here. This is not me. I work so hard to bring these kids to the Lord and Catholics around here don't seem to draw any correlation between their faith and everyday living. Meanwhile, the Assembly of God is offering me a chance to serve the Lord. I need to get out of here!" My fuse was getting very, very short.

Not long after, the bishop of the Diocese of Fargo, Bishop Justin Driscoll, came to Valley City to have what's called an "open service" where he fielded questions and concerns from the people of the diocese. The idea was for people to say, "Bishop, I'm having a problem in this area" or "I have a suggestion in that area" or "Could you answer this question?" I thought perhaps I would tell him my desire to serve in the Church and see if he had any answers for me. Instead, I did something I did not expect.

The place was really packed that night. There were about five hundred people or so. Bishop Driscoll walked in with his miter and vestments to sit on his chair on the edge of the altar area. And as the conversation began and continued, I sat there, just fuming inside. The longer I had tried to be both "born again" and Catholic, the more it had begun to seem to me that there just wasn't any *place* for me inside the Catholic Church. I was twenty-one years old, not very well educated (yet apparently more familiar with the Scriptures than my priest), deeply confused, filled with zeal and love for the Lord, spiritually rejected by my family, at cross purposes with the Church, and, above all, deeply and profoundly angry. I had been around my Evangelical friends, and I was thinking there *should* be a place for me here as there was with them. It was like there was a wall between my sisters and me, my mother and me, my father and me, the Church and me. And as I sat there fuming, I directed more and more of my anger at the Church, thinking *it* was the problem.

So I went to that open service and it was like this magma of frustration and anger came bubbling up and erupted at the Church. I raised my hand, and the bishop gave me the floor. I stood up and said, "Bishop, I'm so frustrated. I gave my life to Jesus and I want to serve Him the rest of my life. I have tried to be a part of the Catholic Church, but there doesn't seem to be a *place* for me. I've tried to teach the Bible, but there doesn't seem to be a place for me there either. The Catholic Church says, 'You're too young.' The Assembly of God says, 'We can use you in youth ministry!' The Catholic Church says, 'You're married.' The Assembly of God says, 'We can use you!' The Catholic Church says, 'You're not educated enough.' The Assembly of God says, 'We'll help you be ordained!'" And as I spoke I became angrier and angrier and I kept talking and talking (while Emily was darting me frantic glances and whispering, "What are you *doing?*"). The more I talked, the more I felt rage toward the religion of my parents well up in me. Finally I stepped into the aisle and shouted, "Sir, I have *had* it with the Catholic Church! I am *done* with the Catholic Church!" The room was stony silent. With my heart about to thump out of my chest, I clapped my hands together, stomped my feet, and said, "From this point on I'm leaving the Catholic Church!" And I turned around and briskly walked down the aisle toward the door, shaking like a leaf and thinking, "Sheesh! I'm going to *Hell* for this!"

However, before I reached the door, I heard the last sound I ever expected to hear:

Clap, Clap, Clap.

I turned around, and it was the bishop, applauding. He stood up, looked at me, and said, "Young man, I want to talk to you later."

I was so embarrassed and upset at what I had done I stammered, "I don't know. I . . . I gotta go to work." And I just left.

Emily slipped out behind me in shock.

That night I thought, "Oh, what have I *done?*" It was the same feeling I'd had when, as a kid, I had accidentally started a fire on the side of our neighbor's house and burned their garage down. I remembered sitting up on a hill and watching the fire trucks come, thinking, "Mortal sin! I've committed a mortal sin!" This was like that. I couldn't sleep that night.

The next morning, I drove my motorcycle out to the convent.

Guess where Bishop Driscoll had spent the night.

I walked in the door that morning and there he was. My face drained of color as he beckoned to me. I thought, "Now he's gonna tell me how long I'm going to be in Hell or how long Purgatory is gonna be for me." I was trembling as we walked into a little room like a confessional. But he just sat down with me, leaned forward, looked me in the eye, and said, "Tell me your story."

So I started to tell him my story of how I grew up in this average Catholic family but never really found a personal relationship with Christ. I poured out my heart about how, when I found a personal relationship and gave my life to Christ, nobody seemed to accept it and everybody seemed to be suspicious of me. I explained how I felt a calling to preach and teach.

When I was finished, I didn't know what to expect. But I will never forget what happened. Bishop Driscoll looked at me with three fingers extended and said, "I'm going to tell you three things. First, I believe what you are doing is of the Lord and that He is leading you."

I asked, "What do you mean?"

He answered, "The search that you are on is of the Lord. The Lord is causing you to seek Him." He went on, "If you wish, I'll write a note to your parents, telling them that."

I appreciated his helpfulness, but I said, "If they won't listen directly to me, I don't know that a note will make them feel any better. Thank you anyway."

Second, he said, "Jeff, I'm going to call you 'Little New-man'."

I didn't know what he was talking about. I thought he might be talking about Alfred E. Neuman from *Mad* magazine. I thought he was calling me a jokester or clown or something.

I said, "What do you mean?"

"Cardinal John Henry Newman," he continued, "was a passionate preacher who converted to the Church. Your zeal reminds me of him. You have that same fight, that same spirit that Cardinal Newman had. He wrestled with his faith and he struggled and God showed Himself to Newman. God's going to do that with you."

Then Bishop Driscoll looked at me with eyes I will never forget and made his third point: "Jeff, there will be a day when you will return to the Church and you will teach your people."

I looked at him for a moment and then shook my head. "I don't think so," I said.

After a short pause, I stood up, sighed, turned, walked out, and never looked back. I left the Catholic Church and I never saw Bishop Driscoll's face again.

Open Door, Shut Door

I continued with my search to find where I felt I could best serve God. I didn't think working at a top forty rock 'n' roll station was the place, even though I had had a chance to talk to many young people. The desire that had been planted in me on that night in February 1977, to preach and teach about Jesus had only grown since then. I wanted to be able to give my whole life to that work, not just squeeze it in between Bee Gees tunes and the weather report. On the other hand, as newlyweds we were still financially rocky and so I remained undecided about what to do next.

Since we had become involved in the local Assembly of God church teaching adult Sunday School, the pastor there wanted to help me get started in learning how to be a pastor. He offered me a position as associate pastor, and we made plans to move next door to the church. As we loaded up our belongings, I received an offer to manage a Christian radio station (KTAV) in Pella, Iowa. I still loved broadcasting, and this appeared to be a good way to be involved with both the Gospel and broadcasting. We were torn on which to choose, but finally we decided to take the radio job and move to Iowa.

Pella is a charming Dutch community which we had passed through on our honeymoon. We had told each other then that we would love to live in a town like that. Each spring the town held a tulip festival where the townfolk would dress in Dutch costumes and scrub the streets clean. The roadsides and parks burst with the vivid colors of tulips. The main square of the town was lined with tall narrow shops that looked like they had come from Holland with the first immigrants. Dutch lace hung in the windows and blue delft ceramics were everywhere. The bakeries could make you gain several pounds just looking in the windows. One of the most popular bumper stickers in the area was "If you ain't Dutch, you ain't much."

Once we settled in and I began work at the radio station, Emily took a job at the Dutch Mill Motel, cleaning rooms. The owners of that hotel, Stan and Judi Van Hemert, listened to KTAV and, as a result, we struck up a friendship that continues to this day. It was through Stan that the Lord began to persuade me, against all my previous experience, that I might have a gift for speaking. It happened this way.

Stan invited me to come give a talk about Jesus in this big back room of his hotel. To my great surprise, people started to come. Then more people started to come. Then a *lot* of people started to come over the next few weeks. To my even greater surprise, I was discovering that I seemed to have a knack for speaking and that it was even getting to be fun! Better still, the response I received from the people was very positive and folks kept coming up to me and saying things like, "You should be a pastor." Oddly, I had never thought of that much in the past — even when I had been given the title "Pastor of Evangelism" back in North Dakota. I had had a dim idea that I wanted to preach and teach, but actual pastoring had never really come into focus for me. Now, however, as people repeatedly suggested it, I just sort of fell into it and thought, "Yeah. If I have a gift for speaking and preaching, this would be the natural place for me to go." I didn't act on this immediately, but the seed was planted.

Now the main denomination in this town was Dutch Reformed while the Catholic Church in that town was very small. For my part, I was not terribly interested in the theology of either of these churches. In fact, I was not interested in theology much at all. That may sound odd given my intense interest in preaching about Jesus and teaching the Bible, but the fact remains that, at that time, I was thinking almost exclusively in terms of "personal relationship" and not in terms of doctrine or theology. Everything was, for me at this point, about being born again, about healing, about revival, and about having an intimate one-on-one relationship with Christ. I just wasn't thinking in terms of Catholic or Calvinist doctrinal questions and answers.

Not surprisingly then, we became involved in an Open Bible Church which is similar to the Assembly of God. They were, after all, thinking along the same lines as I was. They seemed to me to be open to healing and to the gifts of the Holy Spirit. At Open Bible, we made several good friends and Emily and I were encouraged to explore and develop the gifts God had given us for the good of His church.

Meanwhile, my job at the radio station went well for a time, but I found I was too secluded just sitting behind a microphone. I also found it difficult to work for the station owner. I wanted to develop my own type of morning show, but he didn't want it. I found myself chafing under his authority, a problem which re-occurred for me when it came to submitting to male authority figures. Though I wanted male approval, I also did not want to listen to their suggestions. Eventually I left the radio station to manage a gas station. At the gas station I was free to talk with all kinds of people about Jesus. It was right across the street from the college, so naturally students came by for snacks and soft drinks. I would engage them in conversation, and before long the Open Bible Church had several pews filled with excited young people. They were eager to evangelize other students.

As all this was going on, I was still pondering the prospect of becoming a pastor. I didn't know what all was involved with being a pastor, but the conviction grew in me that if I wanted to preach, what better way to do it? Emily and I talked about it, and she felt it was the right direction. So, leaving Emily in Pella, I enrolled in a pastor's training course in Bradenton, Florida, for three months.

The school was called the Institute of Ministry and was a ten-week accredited Bible leadership training school located on the Manatee River. It also served as a retreat center and family camp. Life at school was hard but good. During my first month there, I ate very . . . sparingly. I had no money when I went there and I stayed in a little room in an old man's trailer on the grounds of the retreat center — without air conditioning. Meanwhile, there was a man at school who was a baker and he made what was called "Ezekiel bread." Ezekiel bread was made from ingredients found in the book of Ezekiel. Here's the recipe, in case you have any starving students in your life:

> 2½ cups hard red wheat (winter wheat)
> 1½ cups spelt or rye
> ½ cup hulled barley
> ½ cup millet
> ¼ cup green lentils
> 2 tablespoons great northern beans
> 2 tablespoons red kidney beans
> 2 tablespoons pinto beans

Stir the above ingredients very well. Grind in flour mill (or blender, if sprouted).

Measure into large bowl:

> 4 cups lukewarm water
> 1 cup honey
> ½ cup oil
> 2 tablespoons yeast

Set aside for 3–5 minutes to allow yeast to grow. Add to yeast mixture:

> 2 teaspoons salt
> Fresh milled flour from above mixture of grains.

Stir until well kneaded, about ten minutes. This is a batter type bread and will not form a smooth ball.

Pour dough into greased pans. You may use two large loaf pans or three medium loaf pans or two 9×13" pans. Let rise in a warm place for one hour or until the dough is almost to the top of the pan. If it rises too much it will overflow the pan while baking. Bake at 350° for 45–50 minutes for loaf pans or 35–40 minutes for 9×13" pans.

By the way, if you are fasting (either because you have to as I did, or because you want to), divide the bread into eight equal parts weighing half a pound each. Eat a half-pound cake and drink a quart of water every day. It will, as I discovered, tide you over reasonably well. Also, a lot of people swear by it, saying they have managed to do everything from lose weight to reverse bad heart conditions. I don't know if there is anything to that or not, but I do know it's pretty good bread.

Anyway, this guy baked this bread every day and sold it to me for a dollar a loaf. That was my total food consumption each day for that first month. I didn't want to tell anybody that I didn't have any money. Emily would send me the little bit that she could scrape together, but that wasn't much either. So by the end of the month, I was famished (not to mention kind of tired of the bread). Imagine then, my surprise when the guy who lived with me in the trailer said, "Would you like some steak and eggs tomorrow morning?"

"*Yeah!*" I exclaimed, my mouth watering.

"Great!" he replied. "That'll be five dollars for the steak."

I grinned at him and waited for him to say, "Ju-u-u-ust kidding."

He didn't say it. He was serious.

So I said, "On second thought, I'm not all that hungry. Never mind. Thanks anyway."

Finally, after a month of Ezekiel bread, I brought my hunger to the Lord in prayer and said, "Lord, I need help! I can't go for another two months just eating this bread." One night shortly thereafter, I was sitting in the trailer studying and there was a knock at the door. I opened it and there stood, not a flock of quail, but a Mexican kid who was a student at the school. He was holding a bag of groceries.

I said, "What's this?"

He said, "I was praying and the Lord told me that you needed food. My dad owns a grocery store, so . . . here." He handed me the bag. In it (I'm not exaggerating) there were more than ten steaks, as well as pasta and a whole bunch of other different things! I could not believe it! In fact, I still get choked up over it to this day. There was so much food in there that I wound up tithing it by giving it to some other people who were hungry as well. So, for the next month or so, I had enough to eat and more. Plus, he brought over several more loads of food besides! I will never forget it!

Finally, my time at the school was over. I graduated, returned to Pella, and then was hired as the associate pastor of the Open Bible Church. As a result, I was soon giving more and more talks and Bible studies and was increasingly sought after as a speaker here and there. This was still a new thing for me and I was still at the stage where it was anyone's guess as to whether I might pass out or not in front of an audience. (In fact, one of the three times I passed out in front of an audience was in Pella. I was not Mr. Smooth.)

Still, I felt God was calling me to this and so I kept plugging away, not always with ringing success, but with the steady help and grace of God. One particularly memorable example of God's saving help for me occurred in March 1982. One day, some kids from a local youth group near Pella called and said, "We are in charge of getting a speaker for the Easter service at our church and we were wondering if you would come and address us on Easter morning." I said, "Okay," and marked my calendar.

Easter Sunday rolled around and I headed off to this church. Since it was the youth group that had called I assumed I would be talking to them in the basement of the church or something like that. Like a typical youth minister, I wanted to be hip, casual, and in touch. So I wore jeans and a T-shirt with a big colorful "Jesus loves you" splashed across the front.

I arrived at the church (it had the rather starchy and intimidating name "Ebenezer Reformed"). I was early because they were having a Sunrise Service and I was trying to get there *before* the service. I walked up the main steps and introduced myself to the usher: "Hi! My name's Jeff Cavins and I'm here for the youth. Do you know where I am supposed to be?" I looked around for the steps to the basement.

The usher pointed right up to the main pulpit in the vast, cavernous sanctuary (seating somewhere under one million people) and said, "In there."

I swallowed and licked my dry lips. My eyes locked onto the pulpit and I felt the hair on my neck begin to rise a little.

"W-w-w-well," I said, "w-w-w-where are the youth going to be?"

He said, "The youth will be in there too."

I felt sick to my stomach. In a faint voice I asked, "Where am *I* going to be?"

He said, "In there, of course! You're our guest speaker for the Sunrise Service!"

"For the . . . for . . . you mean, for *everybody?*" I said, suddenly feeling like a salted slug.

"Yeah!"

"Oh God!" I said in panic. I had jeans and a T-shirt on with notes for a five-minute message for youth stuck in one of my ratty pockets. My mind went blank and all I could think to say was, "Oh no! No! I am the *main speaker* for this huge church's Sunday morning Easter service!"

I tried to think. I was half an hour away from home. There was no time for me to get home and change. And even if I did, what would I talk about when I returned? I stood numbly in the vestibule for a few minutes and then wandered in a stupor to the front row of the church. There, I knelt down, opened my Bible, and prayed in desperation, "Oh God, help me! Help me! What am I going to do? I don't have a message and I'm dressed like an idiot!" After several minutes of hyperventilation like this I finally hit on what seemed like a brilliant prayer:

"Lord, let nobody come!"

On Easter Sunday morning.

Fat chance.

After I had finished this dumb prayer, people immediately started pouring in through the door. As the church filled up, the pastor came in and introduced himself. When he took a good look at me in all my well-dressed splendor, his speech was polite but his eyes kept scanning me from head to foot with that "see what the cat dragged in" regard.

Not being a *complete* idiot, I could see what he was thinking and said, "Please! Let me explain!"

When I had told my story, he chuckled, saying, "You'll have to explain that to the people."

I told him I would, but I neglected to mention to him that my message was only five minutes long. I didn't want to increase my chances of passing out in front of the congregation any more than necessary.

So I went back to the front row and sat down. From there, I could look back and see just how badly my prayer had misfired. The place was absolutely *packed*. Meantime, I still didn't have a message. I had no clue what I was supposed to say. So I begged God, "Lord, gimme something! Gimme *something!*" I whipped out my Bible and raced through the concordance in the back looking for words like "Resurrection." Finally, I found a couple of Scriptures that were appropriate. But that's all I had.

By then, it was too late to do any more. The moment had come for me to deliver the message and the minister was introducing me to the now-gigantic congregation. I stood up, walked up to the pulpit, swallowed, and said, "Let me . . . quickly explain why I'm dressed like this."

Then, armed only with the passages from Scripture and shredded rags of my talk for the youth, I started preaching . . . and to my astonishment it ended up being one of the best messages I had ever given. The Holy Spirit came through big time. And I didn't even faint! It was as if God filled my mouth with His words. I spoke about how God wants us to live everyday life with Resurrection power. I had no pause in my thought and the message had focus and clarity. As I stood at the back door to greet the congregation alongside the pastor afterward, many thanked me for the message and also commented how much they "liked my outfit."

After that, I found preaching to be one of the brightest spots in my life. Something about having the Holy Spirit save my neck gave me a renewed confidence that God would indeed be there to help me do the work He was asking me to do. In consequence, I soon found that my speaking, evangelization, and preaching opportunities were really taking off. People were coming to the church from Central College and I had a daily prayer meeting, both of which were new experiences for my church.

On the downside, however, was the depressing world of church politics. And it didn't take long to be exposed to that. One unexpected consequence of my growing popularity as a speaker was that the pastor who had hired me felt increasingly insecure and fell victim to the "Saul Syndrome." I would hold prayer meetings where lots of people showed up. He would hold similar meetings and very few would show. It didn't take long for this kind of thing to become a real strain on our once-tight relationship. As Saul did with David, he began to entertain dark (and completely baseless) suspicions that I was somehow trying to steal his job. Meanwhile, as he was worrying about me, there were other members of the church who really *did* want to get rid of him. It was a classic case of new wine and old wineskins. This group had never really accepted him because they loved his predecessor. So when he attempted to institute a few changes, they fought him every step of the way and at length managed to drive him out.

My poor pastor ended up taking a job at another church several hundred miles away, while I discovered Open Bible Church's unusual method for dealing with pastoral staff: namely, when the senior pastor leaves, the whole staff was suddenly forced to leave as well and a new set of leadership is brought in. On the whole, it was a slightly better arrangement than some of the Old Testament dynastic disputes where, when the king was assassinated, his whole family was exterminated with him. But it still meant that I was fresh out of school, penniless, and jobless (not to mention angry at the people of the church).

Still, at least part of me realized that God had allowed them to shut this door, so I supposed I would have to wait for Him to open another one somewhere else.

From Shut Door to Open Arms

Emily and I wondered what to do next.

As we thought and prayed about it, it seemed to both of us that if God was calling me to be a pastor, and we had no church now, then perhaps He was calling us to plant a church somewhere else. The more I thought about it, the more it seemed to me that it might be possible to do this in Minneapolis. Emily's mother led a Bible study group there that had prayed for us through the years. As we had talked with Mrs. Tobler, she made it clear that this group would be happy to act as our core in planting a church.

Meantime, however, we received word from Pete Weisenberger, who had pastored our old church in North Dakota. He had moved down to Waco, Texas, to plant a church there. Pete called to invite me down to explore the possibility of being associate pastor with him. This seemed promising, so I paid a visit. However, throughout the visit I just did not have a good feeling about it and I could not shake the sense that this was not what God was calling us to do. So I went up to Dallas to meet with a man named Larry Lea. Larry had spent a lot of time around Christ for the Nations Institute and had just begun an exploding new church called the "Church on the Rock" in Rockwall, Texas.

Over lunch with Larry, I asked him to pray for direction about where I should go given these opportunities in the Twin Cities and Waco. We talked and took counsel for quite some time, and it seemed to us that the Holy Spirit was, in fact, calling me to Minneapolis. Finally, Larry laid hands on me and commissioned me to go to the Twin Cities and plant that church. Soon after, Emily's mom and a group of about ten people (in particular, an enormously helpful couple named Dave and Judy Schultz) were busy getting the church incorporated and arranging all the paperwork while we were busy packing our things and moving back to Minneapolis.

The name of our new church was Open Arms Christian Fellowship. Shortly after we arrived we linked up with two other wonderful couples. One of the couples, Mike and Jane Allison, had been in music ministry in Wisconsin. The other couple, Dennis and Kathy Silvers, were from the Rhema Bible Training Center in Broken Arrow, Oklahoma, and we had been introduced to them in Pella. Together, we joined forces to help Open Arms begin. Emily and I thought, "This will be great!" and we plunged into it with all the enthusiasm and joy of people in their mid-20s. It was a lot of work to start the church from the ground up, but we all were excited and felt that this was what we were called to do.

At first, we met in homes, which is where a huge number of nondenominational churches begin. Soon, we started to grow quickly, an exciting interdenominational independent charismatic church. We stayed there for seven years, from 1983 until 1990, pastoring that church, a wonderful church with wonderful people. We were Evangelicals and fundamentalists all coming together to worship the Lord and to study His word. In our time there, we saw a lot of very good fruit. We saw a lot of people come to the Lord. We gave food and clothing to the poor. There were many, many spiritual and corporal works of mercy done there. Our church services were marvelous! You talk about worship! With these people, it was almost like an orchestra! These were quality people!

Sunday morning services had a strongly charismatic flavor. The level of excitement was contagious. Charismatic worship emphasizes the present leading of the Holy Spirit and assumes that if a group of people lays itself open to the power of God, then God will indeed move. Initially, I dimly took this to be in sharp distinction to the Catholic concept of liturgy. I believed that nothing happened every time in the Catholic Mass because I considered it dead ritual. In our charismatic worship, God might burst out at any time with a prophecy, exhortation, or some other supernatural word of power. We regarded our worship services as unstructured and guided solely by the Spirit. This could make things interesting. Every week was a new surprise. We didn't know what we were going to get, or what the sermon might be about, or even what songs we might sing. At first, this could be very exciting. But over the long haul, I found that it tended to lack focus and holy reverence. Occasionally, I still found myself thinking about the more measured approach of the Catholic Church which celebrated the liturgy in a reassuringly predictable way.

A typical worship service on Sunday mornings consisted of a hearty greeting from the minister (and among the various members of the congregation). Then the music minister would say, "Let's all stand and lift our praises to the Lord!" After this would come two or three fast, upbeat worship tunes followed by a little exhortation. Then, the music would slow to a more calm and worshipful tempo and the congregation would enter into a deeper sense of prayer and of their love relationship with Christ. At the end of this, there would typically be a pause as we waited for someone to speak in tongues, or give an interpretation (followed by the predictable applause), or to utter prophecy or praise or a word of knowledge or exhortation. Then we would be seated, there would be an offering, maybe some announcements or a skit or a special song. Then, the pastor would begin the source and summit of the worship service: the Bible study and exposition of Scripture. All this led up to the moment of prayer and ministry during which non-Christians could ask Jesus into their hearts as their personal Lord and Savior, the sick could receive prayer for healing, and/or Christians could rededicate themselves to their relationship with Christ.

As time wore on, I began to notice something about our unstructured worship: it was structured. For despite the fact that we never would have called it by the name, the reality was that this form of worship was every bit as liturgical as anything I ever encountered in the Catholic Church. The structure I have described almost never varied, though the particular content of the words, prophecies, sermons, and so forth were all over the map. I noted this, but then put the thought aside.

As we continued to grow, we had to find larger facilities. Eventually, we rented an elementary school gymnasium every Sunday for worship services (something countless nondenominational church members can relate to). Every Sunday, we would haul everything in and then haul everything back out so that the school could have their gym back on Monday morning. And still we continued to grow.

But mere growth is not an unmixed blessing, as I discovered. One thing that happened during this early period at Open Arms was a phenomenon common to many independent churches in their start-up phase: we started to collect all the odd characters in the area, as well as anyone who was miffed at their previous church.

The odd people ranged in variety quite a bit. A lot of them were people who were not on their medications as they should have been. From these folks we would get periodic outbursts in the middle of the service or announcements that they were computers, not to mention claims (perhaps real) of demonic possession.

The miffed people, on the other hand, were invariably shopping for a new church because "God is telling me to go somewhere else," and they, unfortunately, are now sizing you up with the same sharply critical eye they reserved for their former church(es). These folks tended to come and either spend a lot of time grumbling about their former church or, worse still, transferring their grumbles to our church until the Lord told them it was time to move on again. That could get pretty tiresome, especially since everybody involved in planting the church — including me — was doing the best we could. We were trying to invent a church and we needed help much more than we needed the fault-finding of spiritual gourmets (which is, again, something every independent pastor in the world will tell you).

After two years, the church had grown from twenty people to three hundred. By then, even the gymnasium couldn't hold us so we built a nice sanctuary inside an office warehouse complex. The church ran an outreach center with food and clothing distribution. Several home fellowship groups were held throughout the Twin Cities. A lot of amazing things happened there, but two really stand out in my memory.

There was a Lutheran family that came to our church to visit. This was not unusual, because we had a lot of visitors to our church, especially in the early days. At the end of the service, I offered the opportunity to pray for the sick, which we were accustomed to doing. I invited those who needed prayer to come up to the front. So this visiting Lutheran family came up, a husband and wife and their two little kids.

I said, "How can I pray for you?"

She said, "I've been diagnosed with pancreatic cancer."

I said, "Oh," and my first thought was, "Lord, I was hoping for something more like a cold. I don't know how to pray for cancer."

But as she spoke, her husband burst into tears. He was just overwhelmed with caring for her and two little kids and bearing the burden of it all.

So I said, "Okay." Then, all I did was lay my hand on her and say, "In the name of Jesus. . . ."

She fell down in a heap like a bowl of Jello.

I didn't know what to do. I thought, "Oh no! I've killed her!"

Her family huddled around her and, a few minutes later, she sat up and seemed to be all right. I was greatly relieved.

A few days later, I got a phone call. It was the Lutheran woman.

She said, "You're never gonna guess this!"

"What?" I said.

She said, "I'm *healed*! I got the doctor's report! They did another test and the cancer is completely gone! All of it!"

I couldn't believe it.

She said, "I have all the doctor's reports!" And she proved it by coming to church the next week and bringing them all and showing everyone she had been healed.

She wasn't the only one. On another occasion, there was a girl in the church who was congenitally cross-eyed. She too received prayer and was instantly healed. In fact, we had the thrilling experience of seeing several people receive miraculous healings from the Lord.

Meantime, God was busy doing some healing with Emily and me as well. For the first seven years of our marriage, we had struggled with infertility. We knew the chances of having children were low going into the marriage and so had looked at alternative ideas such as adoption. But, of course, when you are so poor that you have to live on Ezekiel bread for a month you may as well be planning to adopt the Brooklyn Bridge. So we basically resigned ourselves to the idea that if God wanted us to have a child, we would. However, a friend of Emily's who also struggled with infertility had gone to the doctor and was helped, so we finally decided this might be a good idea too. Two months after an amazingly short fertility treatment, she was pregnant (to our great delight). And nine months later, our daughter, Carly, was born on March 30, 1985.

This was a bright spot on the family front because, by this time, the relationship between me and my parents had deteriorated to a silent standoff. They came to our services on occasion, especially if their granddaughter was in a play or concert. But when the topic of conversation turned from Carly's cuteness to anything else, the jabbing started. I would take whatever opportunity presented itself to sneer at the "dead" Catholic Church. They would periodically retaliate with a jab of their own. But this was all guerrilla warfare. My mother never directly asked me why I wouldn't come back to the Church or anything like that. At some point, they had come to realize that, despite their earlier predictions, this was not a phase or a fad. For my dad's part, I even think he was (in spite of himself) able to feel some pride in me because I was a public speaker and, though not a Catholic, still a Christian. This made it easier for him to resign himself to the fact that I was going to be a Protestant pastor.

On the other hand, as a pastor, I had to face the fact of my own weakness and inadequacy on many occasions. Despite the miracles God sometimes chose to work in our midst, we also had one of the first AIDS patients to die in Minnesota at our church, and he was so bitter at the end that he spat at me when I tried to visit him in the hospital. Likewise, I well remember a woman with liver cancer who came to visit our church. She had no husband and two girls at Oral Roberts University. I made up my mind I was going to pray with them and stick with them, no matter what. But despite all our prayers, she went downhill fast and I ended up in a hospital room with her and her two daughters. She entered her death agony and I held her while her two daughters stood by the bed. Finally, she breathed her last and I remember the two daughters looking at me with this expression that cried out, "Do something!"

I felt so helpless. Not only could I not stop people from dying, I felt helpless in many different ways and this increasingly haunted me as time wore on.

It was like this: I was primarily a preacher and teacher. Those were the main gifts the Holy Spirit had given me to exercise and those were the main gifts that had attracted people to Open Arms. Beyond that, people were drawn by the atmosphere of the church. They liked the singing. They liked the music. They liked the praise and worship. And with good reason: the Silvers and Allisons were simply superb. But the longer people were there, the more they began to want something beyond just this. And so, as pastor, I began to have to think of "new" and "exciting" things that would *keep* the people there week after week.

And, of course, all the other independent churches in the
area were doing the same thing. So there began to creep
into everything that I did a little element of ruthless and
Darwinian competition with all the other pastors in the
area. Just where I thought we were going to be getting the
freedom of the Spirit, I found that we (and all the local
independent churches) were getting sucked into a trap of
having to perform or come up with the latest gimmick or
the newest speaker or the latest singer in order to draw
them in and keep them there once we had them. More
and more, my pastoral life was becoming an endless quest
to create the latest hubbub. It was more and more about
feeding a popularity machine and less and less about the
life of the Spirit. Whatever I said about "salvation by grace,
not works" the reality was that my life was becoming a
frantically works-dominated hamster wheel. Worse still, it
all tended to force me to depend on myself alone, because
without my congregation (lured to stay and tithe week after week by our continual spiritual fireworks) I had *nothing*. I could not turn to other pastors for help because they
were the competition, just as I was theirs. On the outside,
there would be a great deal of jovial glad-handing ("Hello
brother! I'll pray for you! Praise the Lord!"). But right below the surface was the constant nagging fear that you had
to keep this guy from stealing your sheep with *his* latest
gimmick, singer, or speaker. I was starting to understand
how my pastor in Pella could have become so paranoid.

   And I was feeling increasingly overworked and in over
my head. As time wore on, I was faced with a problem
inherent in the very nature of what we were attempting
to do at Open Arms: namely, the nagging question: "How
do you start a church from scratch?" It was a dilemma
that greeted us from the first day we met in homes and

remained with me for the next twelve years. I had gifts as a preacher and teacher, but not particularly as an administrator, financial adviser, janitor, counselor, painter, visionary, systems analyst, traffic cop, electrician, plumber, and systematic theologian. Yet I was required to wear all these hats, and many more as well. It was the Peter Principle at work: I had somehow been promoted to my level of incompetence and now I was wondering how I was supposed to reconstruct 2,000 years of history with one Bible? What kind of church government would we have? What kind of discipline? What's the vision of the church? How do you handle finances? Are we going to tithe as a church? How do we organize a diaconate? Shall we baptize infants? Do we pour or dunk? How do we decide such details? *Who are we?* We were doing the best we knew. But there was always the sense that, amid the authentic biblical folding chairs, the genuine apostolic overhead projector, and the worship tunes that Peter and Paul no doubt sang, we were not quite capturing the essence of the New Testament Church. I couldn't shake the sense that we were making this up as we went along.

Worse still, even when we *did* try to do something that seemed to be constructive I was continually confronted with this independent spirit from my fellow believers (not surprising, I suppose, in an independent denomination) that continually greeted every attempt to do something constructive with, "That's not what the Lord is saying to *me*!" Inevitably, this meant that every attempt to do something "according to the clear teaching of Scripture" wound up becoming a contest between individuals claiming to have the best ideas. It also meant a continual barrage of "Our kids aren't really being spiritually fed here," and "My needs are not being met," and the endless stream of pastoral problems that are the daily bread of every independent pastor in the world.

Eventually, such questions forced us to try to come up with a mission statement (which I now recognize to be a sort of watered-down creed). But none of this was very satisfying, and I increasingly wondered how I could get connected with the early Church and see how *they* started and built up churches.

Then, in early 1984, I met a woman named JoAnne Magnuson who introduced me to some tapes by a man named Dwight Pryor. He specialized in what became known as the "Jewish roots movement" and was the president and founder of the Center for Judaic-Christian Studies. This movement aimed at studying Jesus with Jewish eyes and looking into the historical, religious, and cultural background of Jesus. The idea was to understand our faith by looking at it through Hebrew eyes and thereby discover more of what Jesus meant and how the church was to be structured. Jesus, after all, lived in a Jewish world with Jewish customs, grew up as a Jewish child, and His teaching reflected a Jewish background filled with Jewish idioms. The promise of this was that we could actually get into that world and experience the New Testament from a first century Jewish perspective. I could throw away the contact lenses we Protestants had from Calvin, Luther, et al., and see Jesus the way Peter himself did. The more I listened to these tapes, the more engrossing this idea became. I found out, for instance, that Jesus imitated the standard rabbinic methods of teaching in the first century. An example of this was the rabbinic method of teaching called *hekesh* which means "to bang together" two Scriptures in front of the audience. So, when Jesus says, "The son of man came to seek and to save the lost" (Luke 19:10), He is banging together Daniel 7 and Ezekiel 34. Likewise, He employed the rabbinic technique called *remez* or hinting at things rather than saying them outright (as when He hinted at His own divinity when He asked the Pharisees why David called the Messiah "Lord" [Matthew 22:41–45]). By better understanding the world of Jesus, we gain a deeper insight into what the New Testament means. For example, when the Evangelists show us the woman who reached out to touch the hem of His garment (Mark 5:25–34), they know and their readers know she was touching the *tzitzit* on His *talit*, that is, the fringe of His prayer shawl. Since the knots on the fringe were tied in such a way as to represent the 613 commandments of the Torah, her touching of that fringe is an acknowledgment of Jesus' authority, and as the Messiah He is the fulfillment of law.

Aha! This, I thought, was my answer! It was intoxicating! Here was a whole group of people who, it seemed to me, had a clear understanding of the first century Church. Better still, this was a movement taking place among many Protestant churches around the world and affiliated with some very credible academic work among both Christians and Jews such as the Jerusalem School for the Study of the Synoptic Gospels headed by scholars like David Flusser, Shmuel Safrai, and David Bivin. As a pastor, endlessly struggling with the question of how to build a church from the ground up, this seemed to me to be a godsend. So it really became a focus of mine to develop a church that we could call a "New Testament church." I sought a church that would reflect the New Testament Church, going out and preaching the Gospel, laying hands on the sick, and seeing them delivered and healed. Increasingly, it seemed to me that the goal was to understand the first century Church and mimic it. So, in the fall of 1984, I went to Austin, Texas, to spend some time with Dwight. As a result, we found we really hit it off and ended up becoming the best of friends.

As a result of all this, in early 1985, Emily, her mother, and I went on a "familiarization tour" to Israel to study. That trip changed my life. Until then, I had been studying Scripture. Now, I was not only hearing with the hearing of the ear, I was seeing with my own eyes all the places I had read about. For me, to suddenly step onto the soil of Israel was emotionally overwhelming. I had so wanted to go there and now it was a reality! As I stepped off the airplane I was deeply touched to think that this land that I had been studying was now all around me. These were the very places where Jesus had walked! We read the Bible with new understanding. The Bible stories we knew so well could now be imagined in their actual settings: the Jordan where Jesus was baptized, the steps of the Temple Mount, the mountain where King Saul and his sons were killed by the Philistines, the valley where David killed Goliath. I felt as if I belonged in the land of Israel and did not want to return to the United States after a week of touring. In fact, I arranged to stay another week.

I found myself really falling in love with the Jewish roots of the Faith and coming to deeply appreciate the Hebraic perspective on Christianity. Not long after that, I enrolled in Hebrew classes at the University of Minnesota. We founded a Judaic-Christian Study Center (modeled after Dwight Pryor's organization) and started teaching the Jewish roots of Christianity, offering Hebrew courses and leading more trips to Israel. I also began to develop a relationship with Dr. Marvin Wilson at Gordon College, another significant scholar in this movement. I was now firmly convinced that the only way to plant a church was to be rooted in the historic Church. I became ever more convinced that we are a *connected* people.

But the more I came to believe this, the more convinced I became that what we were doing at Open Arms was simply incompatible with that reality. It became more and more obvious to me that the things we were doing in our structure and worship had practically nothing to do with the first century Church. It was a purely late twentieth-century American setup. We had meant well, but we really had been making it up as we went along, interpreting the Bible according to the will of the majority or the most dominant personality. There was practically no connectedness with the Church of history.

Increasingly, I felt much the way I had felt way back in high school and college before I had handed my life over to Christ: I wanted more but I didn't know what I wanted exactly. I wanted more than just preparing sermons on Saturday night, singing songs on Sunday morning, having home groups, and perpetually running on the hamster wheel to keep members. I wanted connectedness, not only with Christ but with His Body as it existed through history back to the beginning of the Church. As a result, I more and more found myself at odds with a lot of charismatic preachers and pastors. It wasn't the people at Open Arms who were the problem. They were some of the most sincere, loving, and godly people I had ever met. In fact, besides Emily's parents, her brother Mark and his wife, Linda, as well as several cousins were faithful members of the church. It was the problem of the independent church's independence from its roots that weighed on me, not the people, who we dearly loved. It was ever more difficult for me to carry on, knowing that we were not engaged with the past.

Charismatic jargon (it's not carefully formulated enough to call it "theology") tends to be dismissive of the mind, the intellect, or of anything to do with formal theology or academic training. Words like "philosophy" or "doctrine" were written off as "head knowledge." Christians who employed these unspiritual words too often were looked on with something like pity as starving sheep who didn't really know the truth (because you can only know the truth "in your spirit"). What "knowing something in the spirit" *meant* was never entirely clear, but it was a phrase we all threw around as though we knew what it meant. In addition, charismatic/pentecostal piety has a strong aversion to anything that smells of "religion." We believed that worship should be "spontaneous" and "unstructured."

As time went on, however, I began to discover that the charismatic/pentecostal suspicion of "head knowledge" increasingly went against the grain of the way God had put me together. I have always been very curious about things and had always wanted to learn more, to understand, to go deeper intellectually as well as spiritually. I wanted to understand — with my mind as far as possible — the divine plan of God in salvation history. It wasn't enough to just *feel* God; I wanted to try to understand Him as much as my puny mind could, to love the Lord my God with all my mind (Luke 10:27). I figured, "God may have given the great theologians minds the size of the Atlantic Ocean and me a mind the size of a thimble, but by golly I at least want my thimble to be full!" And since I was too short to see God clearly when it came to a lot of these issues, I decided to stand on the shoulders of giants. So I started studying the works of various theologians. I studied Hebrew. I studied the Jewish sources of the first, second, and third centuries. Up until now, I had been worshiping God with my heart. Now I was beginning to worship God with my *mind* as well. I was discovering that I could literally read a book and worship God at the same time! Increasingly, my investigations into theology and the Jewish roots movement were becoming a rich source of life to me.

As I studied I began to learn a great deal about the Jewish concepts surrounding worship and also about early Christian theology. As a charismatic/pentecostal Protestant, I had for years believed that all I needed was the Holy Spirit and my Bible. For a long time, I had persuaded myself that such worship was "worshiping God with my spirit" as Jesus had said we should do when He told the Samaritan woman about worshiping God in spirit and truth (John 4:23). Eventually however, something inside had begun to cry out for more. Now as I continued my studies, I began to discover I could not only worship God with my mind, I could worship Him with my body as well.

In a funny way, this was the culmination of something that had begun to dawn on me earlier: namely, that charismatic worship was not as spontaneous as we thought. As I had already begun to notice, a typical charismatic worship service followed the same template in a million nondenominational charismatic or Assembly of God worship services around the world. For in fact, even though we prided ourselves on not being traditional or liturgical, we in fact had our own liturgy and it was as structured as anything in the Mass.

And the more I thought about it and studied Scripture, the more I realized that the problem was not that our worship was liturgical, but that it was not liturgical *enough*. I found that, at a personal level, something within me cried out for rich and deep ways to express my love for God using my whole being, spirit, soul, *and* body. I realized that in any significant relationship we naturally and beautifully do this and, in fact, when we *don't* express our love that love is wounded and crippled. And so, for instance, a husband and wife who never kiss or touch are experiencing not a pure but a *dysfunctional* relationship. Similarly, a relationship between father and child which is purely verbal and never involves physical expressions of love such as hugs or wrestling or birthday cards or gifts or a simple pat on the back is a tragically cold and distant relationship. Our souls, I began to realize, *demand* symbols because our souls are embodied.

Consider, for example, a wedding ring. A wedding ring is not a marriage. Merely putting a wedding ring on does not cause you to be married. But it is a *symbol* of a marriage. We take a piece of metal and attach all kinds of meaning to it. And so, when I am going to a shopping mall and say "hi" to someone, they immediately see the ring and it says something to them: namely, "I'm married." In fact, depending on the other person's circumstances it could mean even more than that. It could mean, "I'm out of bounds. I'm taken. I'm not available." Now if I came up to women on the street and said, "My name is Jeff Cavins and I am in a covenant relationship with a woman from St. Paul, Minnesota, and I have said, 'til death do us part,' and sworn to love, honor, and cherish that woman, so do not get in the way!" they might think me rather odd. Instead, on the day we were married, the priest said, "I want you to wear this little piece of metal as a symbol of all that we're doing here." So I did that, and now I can go out into society and my ring tells the whole story for me symbolically. Indeed, if I take that ring off, lay it on my desk at home, and go out into the world, I am saying something completely different about myself in society. I am saying, in the United

States, "I'm available." I am saying that there is no clear manifestation of my covenant relationship with my wife. That is why, sadly, there are so many men who take off that symbol of the covenant relationship when they go on business trips.

And as with the wedding ring, so with the rest of the wedding. What do you have to do to get ready for that wedding? You need to get a church, a wedding dress, a hall for the reception, license, flowers, best man, bridesmaids, maid of honor, announcements, etc. When the day comes, the two families are seated in different parts of the church. The groom has to stand at the front with the best man, not just hang around chatting until the bride wanders in. And the bride doesn't mosey in from somewhere in the wings wearing jeans and a T-shirt — she comes up the aisle wearing a white dress symbolizing purity. We don't want to see the groom slap the bride on the back and say, "Okay, we're gonna do it. Let's get hitched," followed by somebody at random in the crowd shouting, "You guys wanna be married? Okay, then you're married!"

Our lives are permeated by symbols. When you are driving, the color red means "stop." Red lights have no power whatsoever to stop us, yet the meaning conveyed by the color is still "stop." Likewise, the color green means "go." Similarly, we have many other symbols in our lives. For instance, when I went to college and worked for years for a degree, what happened? Why, when I took my last class, didn't they just say, "Okay, you're done. You took all the classes. Now get out of here"? They could have just said that, but instead they heaped symbol and ceremony on the accomplishment. At the end of that time I went to graduation and wore a funny looking hat and robe. I would never wear such a hat and robe normally, but I did at that moment. Also, I received a little rectangular piece of paper called a diploma. All these things together symbolized the accomplishment. The diploma says, "You have done it! Four years of education! We, the school, honor you with the recognition of a certain degree of education that you've accomplished." And the pattern that is true for graduation is true everywhere: the more precious or important an event, the more symbol and ritual we heap on it.

Likewise, school colors say something about who we are. We go to a football game and see one whole side of the playing field decked out in orange and black because those are the team colors. In fact, symbols are so important that you can go into the wrong neighborhood as a teenager wearing the wrong-colored hat and it could cost you your life. I can go to a football or soccer game in some parts of the world and simply by making the wrong gesture I could spark a riot because that gesture symbolizes something. And so Oscars, Emmys, Tony awards, bowling trophies, blue ribbons, Olympic medals, Congressional Medals of Honor, interior decorating, Christmas trees, birthday candles, and a million other symbols all proclaim one thing in a loud voice: we are people who continually live by symbols and the more important the event, the more we heap symbols upon it.

The ancient Jews did the same. And so, as I studied, I began to discover that Jewish worship was undeniably rooted in *ritual*, *sign*, and *symbol*. In the Temple, all the senses were involved in worship. It was very "thingish" in a way my manner of charismatic worship had not been since I left the Catholic Church. Jewish worship was replete with *things* such as incense for the nose, the *shofar* (the ram's horn blown by the priests) for the ear, the *talit* or prayer shawl for the finger to feel, the altar of sacrifice to

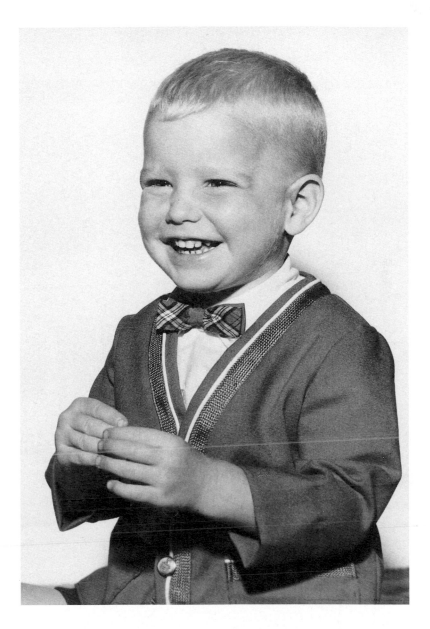

Jeff at age three.

Jeff with father at walleye opening
at Red Lake, Minnesota.

Cavins family 1970: clockwise from
left Trish, Jayne, Jeff, Robert, Leslie.

Confirmation. May 1, 1971.

Jeff as a freshman at Normandale College,
Bloomington, Minnesota.

Emily Tobler when Jeff met her.

Andreas and Alice Tobler, Emily's parents.

Holy Matrimony. June 3, 1978,
Saint Hubert's Catholic Church,
Chanhassen, Minnesota.

Jeff at WCCO Radio, Minneapolis, 1979.

Bishop Justin Driscoll.
Fourteen years as head of the
Fargo (North Dakota) Diocese.

Bishop Paul Dudley, retired bishop,
Diocese of Sioux Falls, South Dakota.

Bishop Robert Carlson,
Diocese of Sioux Falls.

Bishop Andrew McDonald, Diocese of Arkansas.

Jeff is received back into the Church at a Mass in
Jeff's parents' home with Bishop Paul Dudley.
May 27, 1995.

Jeff with Scott Hahn leading a tour to
Israel for Franciscan University.

Jeff on the set with Mother Angelica
before her live show February 28, 1996.

Emily and Carly received into the
Church, April 20, 1996. Also pictured
are Dr. Alan and Nancy Schreck, with
their daughters Margaret and Jeanne.

Jeff with *Life on the Rock* regulars
Jonathan, Rebecca, and Catherine.

Family photo 2000. Clockwise from left are
Emily, Carly, Jaki, and Toni.

see with the eyes, the feasts to taste with the tongue. There were the *mikvah* or ceremonial baptismal immersions, the liturgical rituals involved with praying three times a day, and commemorating feasts at specific points throughout the year. They used precious stones and metals, fine linens, specific colors, oil, water, furniture, tree branches. More-over, they set aside not only things, but space — holy space — and kept it apart from common use. This space in here — within the tabernacle or within the Temple — shall be consecrated to the Lord in a unique way. Likewise, they set aside time as sacred so that not only were aspects of their day, week, or month "uncommon" but their entire year was sacred. All this sprang from the concept of the Sabbath which is, as Rabbi Abraham Joshua Heschel says, "a sanctuary in time."[1] So no matter where you were or what time of the year it was, you were in the process of declaring who God is, His goodness, and who you were in relationship to Him. Old Testament worship, so far from being disembodied, was a feast for the senses. Everything we were studying about early Jewish belief involved not just the spirit, nor just the mind, but the *body* in liturgical ritual, sign, and symbol. Judaism habitually gave *form* to faith. It wasn't just a set of pithy sayings. It was a *way* that gave rhythm to life. It addressed not just the heart, nor just the head, but the *whole* human person as he or she lived life.

What was more, the New Testament did the same. In Romans 12:1, for instance, Paul writes:

I appeal to you therefore, brethren, by the mercies of God,

---

[1] Abraham Joshua Heschel, *I Asked for Wonder: A Spiritual Anthology* (New York: Crossroad, rep. 1992), p. 37.

to present your *bodies* as a living sacrifice, holy and acceptable to God, *which is your spiritual worship*.

Note what Paul does *not* say. He does not say "present your spirits or souls." Rather, he carries over from Judaism the awareness that we are embodied souls or ensouled bodies. For him, "spiritual worship" means presenting our bodies to God. And "present" in Greek means "a ritual presentation of a sacrifice."

That caught my attention. We are to come in a ritual fashion and offer our bodies. Also attention-getting was the word in that passage (*latreia*) which we translate as "worship." When the Old Testament was translated into Greek (in what is known as the Septuagint version) they used this word to describe the service and worship of God according to the requirements of the Levitical law. Likewise, Paul himself uses the word elsewhere (in Romans 9:4) to describe the worship offered by Israel in the Temple. Of all the terms used to describe worship in the Old Testament, Paul now uses *this* word to describe how we must present ourselves to God. And as I read further, I began to see in Scripture how this pattern of bodily offering sprang from liturgical roots.

For, as the whole Jewish roots movement was showing me, our Christianity has its roots in the Old Testament. Jesus didn't begin something novel; He came to fulfill what had already been established (Matthew 5:17). So we Christians are linked to Israel. And what do we find in Israel's Scriptures in terms of worship? We find Moses bringing incredible order and form to worship. There is a prescribed method of worship that says, "Do this on this date. Dress this way. This person does this and that person does that. Here is how you bless, etc." In the same way, during the reign of David we see the introduction of great "orchestras" to be used in public worship. And during the Babylonian Captivity, the Jews developed the synagogue where prayers were prescribed on a daily and seasonal basis. Prayer was, itself, highly public and liturgical. There were set orders of readings, responses, and singing of psalms. There were seasons, feasts, prescribed sacrifices, and regulations on relationships. In fact, it was so incredibly ordered and so very little was left to chance that I doubt many people today would look at that as a kind of religion they would want to belong to. But still, there it was in Scripture. And so I wondered, if we consistently find a form given to worship in Hebrew Scripture, is it alien to Christianity to expect the same thing in the new covenant form of worship? I began to realize that we were inventing forms of liturgical prayer such as twenty-four-hour prayer chains, but denying the underlying principle that we are liturgical beings.

Before coming to this realization, my theology was partly influenced by a popular charismatic interpretation of Colossians 2:16–17: "Therefore let no one pass judgment on you in questions of food and drink or with regard to a festival or new moon or Sabbath. These are only a shadow of what is to come; but the substance belongs to Christ." I had long been taught that this meant, in essence, that the Old Testament was a religion that believed in outward form but New Testament worship was "spiritual" and therefore inward, formless, and bodiless. But as I began to read the New Testament in light of the Old Testament's insistence on a liturgical form for worship, I discovered this was not so. For the fact is a) the Old Testament is not a religion of soulless externalism and b) Jesus did not differ from the pattern given in the Old Testament.

The Old Testament is not a religion of soulless externalism for the obvious reason that it, as much as the New Testament, insists not merely on outward show but on the fact that "you shall love the Lord your God with all your heart, and with your soul, and with all your might" (Deuteronomy 6:5). The writers of the Old Testament did not regard the law as a set of obstacles impeding freedom of worship. Rather, they saw it for what it was: guidance intended to lead them, from cradle to grave, *into* freedom. The word "Torah" comes from the root word *yarah* which is derived from an archery term meaning "to hit the mark" and the mark is righteousness, freedom, and happiness in the Lord. It is true that, because of sin, they did not end up being free. But that was not the fault of the guidance. So the idea of giving form to worship remained a good thing, however badly Israel failed to profit from it.

That is why Jesus never criticized or questioned the idea of liturgical worship that was part of Israel's heritage. Rather, we see that He celebrated the feasts and liturgies of Israel and, at the Last Supper, Jesus followed the prescribed liturgy for the Passover. He agreed with all that went before Him by being a part of it and fully entering into it, while at the same time revealing its full meaning. What is more, He taught His apostles to do the same. That is why Paul says in 1 Corinthians 14:40 that "all things should be done decently and in order."

Of course, all the time I'm discovering all this, I'm thinking about how for all these years I've been teaching that we're "delivered" from that "liturgical excess." But my charismatic tendency to distrust and fear anything that looked like form or liturgy was wavering under the sheer beauty and weight of the biblical evidence in favor of worshiping God using ritual, sign, and symbol. And that presented me with a problem that continued to nag at me:

namely, as independent charismatics, we were not observing any particular calendar or any particular form of worship. We were just waiting on the Holy Spirit to see what random thing God might want to do today. Increasingly, it was becoming obvious to me that this was profoundly inconsistent with the entire history of God's people. Facing that was hard. I didn't know what to do. I was hungry for liturgy in a non-liturgical church. I wanted to express my love for God with more than words. I wanted to be connected to the people of God through history and yet I was pastoring an independent congregation. Where was I supposed to go?

And then, in 1989, I heard from Dwight Pryor again. He had relocated his ministry to Dayton, Ohio, and told me there was an opening in the nearby town of Xenia with a group of people who were looking for a pastor and were interested in Israel and the Jewish roots movement. All of this was extremely exciting and I thought, "This is it!" I thought for certain that I was finally at bedrock and that I could hear Jesus (and the New Testament teaching on how to build a church biblically) in this way. Plus, this was not only a chance to pastor a church that appeared to be in agreement on the concept of the Hebraic church, it was also a golden opportunity to work closely with my friend and mentor, Dwight. So in January 1990, we parted amicably with Open Arms and moved to Xenia, Ohio, full of fire, and started meetings on how we were going to develop an authentic New Testament church.

We had the best intentions.

High Hopes and New Discoveries

The day we left Minnesota, the air was almost eighty degrees below zero with the wind chill factor. But when we arrived in Xenia, the air was full of the sense of excitement. We were leaving the little dream home we had just built the year before, but we didn't mind. This was a bigger dream! The chance to pastor a church with people who were serious about building a New Testament life, serious about scholarship, serious about Hebrew and the Jewish roots of the Christian faith! We felt as though we stood before a canvas with nothing on it and that we could create any type of church we wanted to! We sincerely believed we had reached that apostolic bedrock and that looking at Jesus from the Hebraic perspective was the key to it all. On top of this was the normal excitement and anticipation that greets any pastor coming to a church. A large number of people from the church greeted us with great warmth and we felt extremely welcomed by them. We were enveloped in a tremendous sense of brotherhood and family by these kind people.

The church in Xenia was called "New Covenant Fellowship." It was a small church which met (as Open Arms did) in a warehouse. (Meeting in places like warehouses and gymnasiums is, by the way, not particularly unusual in the nondenominational sectors of Christianity. For some, in fact, it is something of a point of pride: it's less "religious," you know.)

The church was run by elders (Dwight was one of these,

a teaching elder) and there was a plurality of leadership with the pastoral duties of weddings, funerals, visitations, and preaching falling to the senior pastor. New Covenant Fellowship was a profoundly *giving* church. They had a beautiful heart for missions and did a lot of wonderful things, including mission trips to Russia to preach in the high schools. As a result, I had the opportunity to preach the gospel in downtown Moscow (both before and after the fall of Communism in Russia). That was exhilarating! I will never forget the time three fourths of a Russian high school student body came forward in tears at an altar call to give their lives to Christ as their Savior. At that same meeting, the principal of the high school walked up to me in front of the entire student body, began to weep, and with outstretched arms asked, "Could I please have a Bible?"

In addition, NCF was chock-full of talent. Dwight and his wife, Jeanette, had an international teaching ministry. For me personally, my friendship with Dwight was one of the most profound things to ever happen to me. There have only been two or three people in my whole life who exhibited the kind of incredible integrity that Dwight exhibits. He is a man who hungers to know Christ and to know the truth. I had, have, and always will have the utmost respect for him.

We also had a wonderful music ministry and a group of people very gifted at leading worship. Some of these led liturgical dance in our worship services (patterned, of course, after the worshipful dance David offered to God before the Ark of the Covenant [2 Samuel 6:14]). Our worship was similar to the way things had been done at Open Arms, but with this significant difference: we paid attention to the Jewish liturgical calendar and tried to celebrate our worship in light of it. This was, for me, deeply exciting and fulfilling because, for the first time as a Protestant, I was experiencing worship using ritual, sign, and symbol and discovering the reality that, so far from imprisoning me, it really was giving life order and rhythm. Rather than worship consisting of just me sitting outside of a living tradition and trying to make things up as I went along based on whatever happened to pop into my head that day, we actually had a form going way back to the Old Testament. Rather than trying to invent something for myself, I could ride along on the back of this tradition. Further, as time progressed, we made more trips to Israel where members of our church were involved in dance and processions during the Feast of Tabernacles celebrations in Jerusalem. In fact, one couple from our church was responsible (for several years) for feeding Christian pilgrims during that Feast at an annual dinner held in Qumran, where the Dead Sea Scrolls were found.

But above all, the greatest glory of NCF was the deep hunger and zeal of that church to *learn*. These people were *disciples*. They were people who, on their own, would learn Hebrew. They were people who would come for any special event that our church held. They were people who gave with no expectation of reward. They were people who would reach out and witness to the Gospel. They were exuberant in worship and could give themselves to an hour and a half of praise and prayer with delight. They were, in a word, people with *life*.

Not surprisingly then, New Covenant Fellowship began to grow. People were intrigued by the Hebraic perspective of our church and more and more of them began to come to our services and hear what we were talking about. Sermons went well, ministries grew, and my studies continued.

One problem that I began to give a lot of thought to was

the question of what worship with ritual, sign, and symbol ought to look like in light of the Resurrection of Christ. After all, the Jewish emphasis on giving form to worship, though it was not scrapped by Jesus, was indeed transfigured by Him. Jesus didn't simply abolish the Passover meal at the Last Supper, but He did give it a whole new meaning. So how were we supposed to celebrate using ritual, sign, and symbol in a way that was appropriate now that the Resurrection was no longer in the future but in the past?

My big clue was the Incarnation and Resurrection of Jesus Christ Himself. God the Creator and Author of time, space, matter — this very "thingish" God — is also God the Redeemer. The One who employed so many appeals to the senses in the Old Testament to communicate His love and truth did not, in the New Testament, suddenly start demanding that salvation be communicated to us simply and solely by means of a high philosophical conversation. Rather, He took on a physical, carbon-based body made of the same blood, muscle, nerve, and digestive tissues as you and me and lived a completely human life. What is more, after His death, He did not just dissolve back into disembodied "spirituality." He was raised — bodily. So the Old Testament Jews were not simply off on a wild goose chase in the reverence with which they treated created things such as the human body or the Ark of the Covenant. They were being led (though some did not realize it) to the ultimate honor given to created things when God the Son took on a human body and raised it to sit at the right hand of God the Father.

In the same way, the Jewish habit of setting aside a particular place as a place of worship was another kind of anticipation of Christ. For when God came to earth in the person of Jesus of Nazareth He did not announce vaguely, "I'm here . . . somewhere!" He refused to remain diffuse and cosmic. He became a specific baby laying in a specific manger in a particular village, born of a specific family and having these particular parents. As C. S. Lewis said, "The world which would not know Him as present everywhere was saved by His becoming *local*."[1]

Likewise, what He did for space He did for time: He consecrated it and set it apart. He was born, lived, died, and rose, not just any old time but "in the fullness of time" (Galatians 4:4). He lived, not "once upon a time" but during the tenure of a Roman prefect whose reign can be pinned down pretty closely in the historical records. And by entering time, as by entering space and matter, Christ *hallowed* it and raised it to participate in His risen life.

And so, our sins were dealt with how? In a *body*. As Hebrews 10:5 says: "When Christ came into the world, he said, 'Sacrifices and offerings thou has not desired, but a body thou hast prepared for me.'" It was by that body made of real flesh and by His real, red, wet, physical blood — not simply "spiritually" — that Jesus purchased our eternal redemption. And it happened not everywhere and nowhere, but *in a specific physical place and at a specific historic time*. And when He ascended (bodily) He did so with the promise that He would come back for us and for "the redemption of our bodies" (Romans 8:23) when it was all said and done at the end of this world.

So this was the wonder of all wonders: the Incarnation! The Word made, not word, but *flesh* and entering fully

---

[1] C. S. Lewis, *Miracles* (New York: Macmillan Publishing, 1947), p. 147.

and even zestfully into the thingishness of this world by taking on a body of matter Himself and taking not only that body but us and creation itself to be with Him in the new Heaven and new earth (Revelation 21:1). So the New Covenant is not to be disembodied. On the contrary, the idea that "spiritual" equals "disembodied" is one that comes, not from Scripture, but from Platonic dualism or gnosticism.

Platonism is a philosophy that holds to a dualistic world-view: the visible material, which is believed to be the source of evil, is in tension with the spiritual, the real home of the soul. In this philosophy the individual is continually trying to escape the material world to experience the bliss that only comes from the spiritual world. The Gnostics, who further developed Platonism, taught that salvation was obtained by escaping the body through esoteric knowledge.

Some Christians do not know this however and go around using slogans and catch phrases like "I am a spirit, I have a soul, and I live in a body." This sort of woolly phraseology tends to encourage the idea that the body is a sort of disposable Tupperware container rather than something essential to our humanness. And this, in turn, tends to encourage the idea among many Christians that the unseen and disembodied "spiritual world" is the real world and even the "good" world, while the created world is bad and unspiritual. The practical upshot of all this is the blurry notion that anything to do with my body or my humanness cannot be right and must be intrinsically evil. Many ancient Greeks took exactly this view and had a saying: "The body is a tomb." But ancient Hebrews, following Genesis, thought the world was good. Instead of fleeing the world, they believed we experience God's fellowship, love, and saving power in and through creation. Christian-

ity, following this divine pattern, teaches that, though soul
and body can be distinguished, they were never intended to
be divided. That is why, for instance, Paul prays that God
may sanctify His people "wholly," with not only "spirit and
soul" but "*body*" kept sound and blameless at the Lord's
coming (1 Thessalonians 5:23). He knows, as does historic
Christianity after him, that the distinction between body,
soul, and spirit is not a license to stop being believers in
the divine pattern and start being Platonic dualists. Spirit,
soul, and body are intended to be *whole*, not divided.

Not, of course, that body and spirit *can't* be so divided.
But in historic Christian theology, the technical term for
such division is not "spiritual purity," but "death." When
body and spirit are ripped apart you do not have a healthy
human being in full spiritual flower; you have a corpse
and a ghost. Christianity alone has the remedy for this: the
Resurrection. For in the Resurrection body and spirit are
reunited and the division, introduced not by Christ but by
the sin of Adam, is finally healed. Creation — all of it and
not just our spirits — is redeemed in Christ because God
has entered into creation itself and joined it to Him by
becoming a creature Himself.

But this confronted me with something I had not thought
of before. Up until now, we had been working with signs
and symbols which *represented* something about God. But
in the mystery of the Incarnation something bigger is going on. For Jesus isn't just a symbol of God: He *is* God!
In Him, matter such as His Body and Blood didn't just
symbolize something about God, they *were* the Body and
Blood of God incarnate. And realizing that, I realized that
Jesus could not merely be spoken of as a sign. Rather, Jesus
Christ is the *sacrament* of the Father. Jesus said to Philip
in John 14:9, "He who has seen me has seen the Father."

If you look at Jesus, you're looking at the Father. Jesus is here to give us the Father, not a symbol of the Father, not a description of the Father, but the Father Himself. Meet Jesus and you have met the Father. That is why Jesus says, "I and the Father are one" (John 10:30). So when you shake hands with Jesus, you're coming into direct contact with God Almighty.

Realizing this, I began to see that *the Church is a sacrament of Christ*. For over and over in Scripture, Jesus very deliberately and consciously identified the members of His body with Himself just as He identified Himself with the Father. He did it in Matthew 25:40 when He said, "As you did it to one of the least of these my brethren, you did it to me." He did it when He said to Saul (who was persecuting Christians, not Jesus personally), "Saul, Saul, why do you persecute *me?*" (Acts 9:4). And He did it when He told the apostles, "He who hears you hears me, and He who rejects you rejects me, and He who rejects me rejects Him who sent me" (Luke 10:16). In all this, it began to become clear to me that the Church — the body of Christ — is not just a symbol of Christ. It is not some kind of memory jogger so society will recall Jesus from time to time. Rather, we *meet* Christ in the Church and in each of her members. That is why Jesus told His disciples to announce that the kingdom of Heaven had come to your door and my door. For we are His body. His life is living within us. So when we go out and knock on doors or shake hands with somebody or help someone who's broken and hurting, we can do that in the confidence that, just as Jesus is a sacrament of the Father so we are a sacrament of Christ. We are going out into the world and giving His life to other people.

That started me thinking about sacraments a great deal. And that, in turn, prepared me (which is to say defenseless) for a conversation I had with my dad one day in 1992 at a Wendy's restaurant. Things were still uncomfortable with my parents. As we did every Christmas, we made the journey to Minnesota to be with our families. But it was often fairly unpleasant. Our daughter Carly was their only grandchild and they loved to be with her, but I was still in the habit of making jabs and sharp remarks about their Catholicism. So as we sat down to eat that day I was still a rather disagreeable table guest for my parents. My now-ingrained habit was to pick out some oddity in the news, some cult or bizarre thing, and then connect it to the Catholic Church. I would say things like, "D'ja hear about the weird cult in Indiana? They practiced celibacy! Just goes to show you where *that* leads. No wonder that priest was arrested for abusing kids the other day. When you don't stick to the Scriptures you're just headed for trouble. That's what happens when you have a church like the Catholic Church that's just built on empty traditions of men and not the word of God." I did this all the time with my parents and this day at Wendy's was no different. I plugged some of my standard conversational tapes into the speech center of my brain and just let fly about "dead religion" and "rituals of men" that were "unbiblical." It was more out of habit than anything else, especially since my studies had begun to call into question a lot of this sort of rhetoric about ritual and tradition. But, of course, it still bugged my dad and that was the main thing I was after at that moment.

And it worked. My dad was perturbed by my tone of voice and the canned quality of my remarks and he finally replied, "I read my Bible, too, Jeff, but I don't talk about it to everyone all the time. We *are* Christians, too, you know." His voice was low and even and something in him was very serious and intelligent. Then, he dropped what was, for me, at that point in my life and studies, a bombshell: "Tell me something: if you believe the Bible, why don't you believe what Jesus said when He told the disciples, 'This is my body'?"

I blinked. "That's not actually what He meant," I countered. I was about to begin my explanation that I had been taught way back in my charismatic and pentecostal Bible college days ("Jesus was speaking spiritually and we don't experience God through crude physical things yaddayadda-yaddayadda. . ."), but I didn't have any conviction behind my words. I sort of fumbled around looking for something to say that would let me win the argument but not betray what I was learning in my studies. I could think of nothing. I felt my upper lip get a little sweaty.

"How can you say you believe the Bible literally but you won't accept that? I don't understand how you can do that," my father said.

I did not have a response to give and he knew it.

I don't remember the rest of the conversation, but I was acutely aware after this that he was asking a question I'd been coming ever nearer to asking myself. If God could join Himself to matter, space, and time in the physical body of Jesus Christ, why would it be impossible for Him to change the bread and wine into His Body and Blood? It was a question that stuck in my craw and a seed that took root inside me, but it would take some time to get above the soil.

For I could not acknowledge to him — my unspiritual dad — that he had a very good point. So I tried to shelve the question (without success) and refocus my thoughts on New Covenant Fellowship. After all, we had Scripture and we had rootedness in the liturgical tradition of Israel. We understood the biblical insistence on giving form to worship through ritual, sign, and symbol. I was even beginning to appreciate the sacramental ideas of the early Christian Church. So what else did we really need? I decided I'd go back to the elders and suggest having communion more frequently. *That* would show dad I took communion seriously. And besides, even if my dad had (maybe) said something that was on the ball here, we were still doing pretty darned good as a church.

So, after more study to find out whether Jesus and the apostles really had this strong emphasis on regular celebration of Communion, I urged the elders who helped guide the church to make the Lord's Supper a weekly event and put more importance upon it. They all seemed to think it was a good idea, so we started to partake of communion every week. It was still regarded by us as a symbol, not a sacrament, and certainly not as the Body and Blood of Christ, but it was regarded with great reverence. All seemed well and the challenge posed by my dad seemed to fade as the church grew and grew. In fact, the day finally arrived in 1993 when I announced that I wanted to see the church grow into a Dayton citywide church (as I had told them when they had hired me). My goal was to have evangelization efforts that could possibly mean moving the church from the small city of Xenia to Dayton proper.

I had no idea at the time, but that was the beginning of big trouble.

Changes

In making that announcement I began to run into a fact of life encountered by countless independent pastors around the world. That fact of life was this: Any time a pastor wants to take a church in a new direction, there are two things that happen: 1) his initiative is greeted very warmly by some people because they are very excited to have a new pastor; and 2) others in the church are suspicious of the pastor (and usually these folks are the ones who ran off the previous pastor).

In the particular case of NCF, the congregation had gone through some tough times before my arrival. The senior pastor who preceded me had fallen into various difficulties and there was some healing that had to take place as a result. But the healing left scars. One of those scars would eventually manifest itself in the fact that some of the church founders — many of whom were elders — were very adamant that the church *must* stay in Xenia. However, no one had conveyed this to me when I took the job. In fact, several of the elders had said they were open to growth, evangelization, expansion, and even to the possibility of moving to Dayton.

The reality, however, was that the original members of the church weren't. There was, in fact, an animosity toward the people from Dayton who were increasingly filling the pews of the church. These new people upset the apple cart and forced the folks from Xenia to begin to think and do things in new ways. Being new myself, this seemed great to me, but many of the elders did not share my enthusiasm. They felt threatened by all these newcomers and by the plans I was making to bring even more of these people into the church. (Looking back on it now, it reminds me of the conflict between Hebrew-speaking Jews and Greek-speaking Jews in Acts 6. Turf wars are nothing new in the history of the Church.) So this conflict lay silent but operative below the surface of New Covenant Fellowship. And I was clueless about its existence.

It began to surface with the arrival of a new couple at the church. The Joneses (not their real names) had genuinely warm and loving personalities. But (and this is particularly a pitfall in charismatic congregations) they had a way of conveying to people — warmly and lovingly, of course — that they were in continuous and direct contact with "The Voice of the Lord." As a result, their popularity and influence grew by leaps and bounds. People would go to them for prayer and "prophetic guidance" and they endeared themselves to a large portion of the congregation (including me) very quickly. They became my friends.

But then they started to point out problems that they saw with the Jewish roots movement. Well and good, I thought. I didn't agree with them, but figured that everyone is entitled to an opinion. However, over about a year's time another dynamic kicked in that I did not foresee: namely, the group of people from Xenia who feared and resisted moving to Dayton began to make common cause with the Joneses because they both had one thing they agreed on: they disagreed with me. And so the Joneses were taken under the wing of this group and groomed and molded into their champions and spokespersons against me in a concerted campaign to keep the church in Xenia.

So here we were, perched on the verge of explosive

growth and there suddenly arose — to my complete surprise — this ever-more-pronounced note of discontent and
dissatisfaction from the Xenia folks. I would like to say I
was a saint and took it all in stride, but the reality was
it really hurt. Up to this point, I had married their children, buried their fathers and mothers, visited their sick
in hospitals, prayed for them, taught, and been there for
them in every way that I knew how to be of help. Yet now,
suddenly, people from Xenia are starting to complain, in
whispers, that "the pastor doesn't care about us." They are
saying more and more loudly that I'm not with them, that
I only care about the Dayton people. It felt the way a father
would feel if he came home and was met at the door by
his children saying, "We don't think you *are* our father!"

I was troubled by this. At first, I thought the dissatisfaction could be ministered to if I met with the elders and
we sat and talked the thing through. But I found that, no
matter what I did, the dissatisfaction continued to grow.
Then I started to discover that the Joneses were meeting
on a regular basis with the elders who headed the Xenia
faction and actually discussing a church split! They were
discussing, in fact, the idea of pastoring the church in Xenia
and making me pastor of a Dayton church. I confronted
them about it and they flatly denied any such plan was in
the works. However, later it came out that they had, in
fact, been discussing exactly this.

The upshot of all this was that NCF became ever more
embroiled in a nasty and vicious divisiveness resulting in
a large number of personal attacks on me, my faith, and
my integrity. And most painful, much of this was articu-
lated by the Joneses, whom I had trusted and befriended,
yet who, when I came to think of it, had just blown into
town one day, without theological training, with nothing

in the way of credentials, and with nothing more than a warm smile and a personal insistence that they were God's mouthpieces.

I had never been part of a church split in my life, even though I had talked to many pastors who had been through one. But as the five-year stay went on in Xenia, and this (admittedly minor in the grand scheme of things but still excruciatingly painful) example of petty church politics played itself out, I started to grow more and more disenchanted with the independent church movement. Half of the elders (including Dwight) supported me, the other half sided with the disgruntled folks. And as I was now painfully discovering, we were caught in chaos of our own making. There was simply no ecclesial structure with which to deal with this, no authoritative tribunal that could do an investigation of the various claims and counterclaims or render a judgment of the situation. And the result, so far from being a theological abstraction, was a real human cost in real tears and pain.

As time went on, Emily and I thought more and more about this problem. At Open Arms I had begun to realize the need for connectedness with the historic Church and with our roots in the past. New Covenant Fellowship had, with its emphasis on Jewish roots, answered that need and, as result, our worship of Christ and our practice of the faith was all the richer. But this rich combination of Scripture and rootedness in Judaism was, I was now finding, not enough. For the irony of the situation was that, though we were extremely familiar with our Jewish roots, we were still almost completely ignorant of our Christian roots. For all our interest in getting connected with the Old Testament, as an independent church, there remained a real sense of isolation and unconnectedness from the historical Church. We knew almost nothing about Catholic, Orthodox, or Reformation history and theology. We were a group of people who were excited about the Lord but largely disillusioned with traditional expressions of Christianity. So we had left our Lutheran, Methodist, Catholic, Baptist, and other churches in search of something purer. As a consequence, anything that smacked of ecclesial *authority* was instinctively and reflexively rejected as synonymous with *authoritarianism*.

Now I was beginning to study Scripture again and rethink that. I was coming to realize that true, healthy authority was, in fact, the only thing that kept authoritarianism at bay. After all, in Acts 6, when the Greek-speaking and Hebrew-speaking Jews quarreled, there was an authority (the apostles) who could render a just judgment and take practical steps to resolve the conflict. But when this conflict erupted at NCF, where, I wondered, was that authority? As time went on, I found myself fighting a growing sense of despair over Christ's Body. I would speak with other pastors who were going through very similar things and seek their wisdom and insight. But they had no more clues than I did. We were like drowning men all clutching at one another. I remember one night I just broke down weeping and thinking, "Lord! Where will I go? Who can I go to if I cannot trust your *Body*?" There was no firm place for my foot, nothing solid to grasp, and no one had any light to shed on my darkness. What do you do when someone says, "The Lord told *me*. . . ." How do you answer that? Increasingly, it became obvious to me that, in an independent church, there *isn't* any answer to that. The only reply was the equally subjective, "Well, the Lord's not saying that to *me*." Everything becomes "he saith/she saith." And the practical result of that in any question of importance was that everything turns into nothing more than a raw struggle for power and the truly authoritarian imposition of the will of the winner. Yet it increasingly seemed to me that none of us — including me — *had* any real authority. The apostles had their authority from Christ and Christ had His from God the Father. Where did we — where did I — get authority?

This question of authority continued to bug me more, especially as we continued — ironically — celebrating frequent communion as I had suggested we do. There was, of course, the inherent weirdness of celebrating communion as the "one body of Christ" even while we tore that body to pieces. But in the back of my mind, there was also the question that continued to haunt me: Were we supposed to be partaking of a *symbol* or a *sacrament*? Did Christ give His Church mere signs that remind us of Him or a sacramental extension of His incarnate power that communicates His life to us in the aftermath of the Resurrection? And was that, as Romans 12:1 and the other Scriptures I mentioned previously strongly suggested, a liturgical participation in Christ's sacrifice?

All this led me, while still continuing to fulfill my pastoral duties at NCF, to start studying the "Convergence Movement" in 1993. This was a movement that Professor Robert Webber of Wheaton College talked about which brings together the Evangelical, liturgical, and charismatic aspects of Christianity into a sweet blend. He explained how it combined the stability of the liturgy with the excitement of the charismatic and the zeal of the evangelical world. That really excited me! Their goal was exactly what I was looking for: taking the best of all these worlds and putting them together in a way that honored all that was good in them. Odd as it may sound (what with my having been raised Catholic and all) this represented the first time, for me, that I had ever noticed anyone taking the Jewish concepts of liturgy and symbol into Christianity and making them *sacramental* in union with the risen Christ. It was also the first time I heard of anyone doing this and still having the freedom of the Spirit.

The most famous expression of this movement was the Charismatic Episcopal Church. This was a church in communion with the Anglican and Episcopal churches, yet which incorporated charismatic worship and Evangelical lifestyle with the sacramental and liturgical traditions of the Anglican way. It was one of the fastest-growing, most dynamic churches in the country. It had been featured in *Charisma* magazine and was clearly open to both the power of the Holy Spirit and yet submissive to ancient tradition. Plus, there was a beautiful tradition of study in the Episcopalian and Anglican churches that appealed to me as well. Great writers like C. S. Lewis and Dorothy L. Sayers were Anglicans and the church has a long and rich heritage going back centuries. I was very excited by all this and decided to investigate further.

In the course of my investigation, I met a man named Ken Talle, who headed up a liturgical dance workshop. I came to know Ken. He was a member of the Romanian Orthodox Church and he helped me understand much more clearly the beauty and power of liturgical worship that was rooted not only in sign and symbol (as Jewish worship is), but also in the sacraments of Jesus Christ which not only represent Him, but actually communicate His life and power to us. The beauty of the ancient Christian liturgies was that you could *enter into* them, rather than have to make them up yourself. The liturgy was provided for you and so you could focus on Christ and not waste time reinventing the wheel. This too was deeply attractive.

Another very helpful person was Randall Bane, a deacon in the Charismatic Episcopal Church who lived in Kansas City. He invited me to come to Chicago, to Wheaton College, to participate in a seminar with him featuring Robert Webber. So I went and had the opportunity to meet Dr. Webber and discuss his book *Signs of Wonder: The Phenomenon of Convergence in Modern Liturgical and Charismatic Churches*. We had a long talk about liturgy and the upshot was that I came away hungrier than ever for both liturgical/sacramental worship and the Evangelical fire I had found in the charismatic/pentecostal sector of Christianity. Everything seemed to be pointing me in this direction and helping me come to these conclusions.

Meantime, back in Dayton, I'm still trying to introduce all these new ideas about sacramentality and the ancient *Christian* liturgical tradition into our worship, as well as work out my own situation with the church. But I was deeply uncertain about what, exactly, I should be doing and why, exactly, I had the authority to do it. At the most visible level, that uncertainty expressed itself in various and sundry attempts to offer stopgap patches to our form of worship. In addition to frequent communion, I eventually incorporated a time for us to recite the Apostles' Creed. Also, we began to have different readers come up and offer three readings from Scriptures. I wasn't conscious of it at the time, but this was an imitation of the Liturgy of the Word during Mass. I started to have candles burning in the sanctuary during worship. I tried other tweaks and adjustments in an increasingly restless confusion over how to make our worship more sacramental. And, of course, in our wounded atmosphere — this was all going on during the time of my conflicts with the Joneses and their followers — some people felt threatened by this and feared that we were losing our freedom and becoming "religious." In fact, I met with sufficient resistance to tell me it wasn't a good idea in such a raw emotional situation and backed off. Besides, all of these adjustments were insufficient, because they didn't address the central issue which was increasingly coming to dominate my heart and mind.

That issue was the question of what Jesus meant at the Last Supper when He instituted Holy Communion. Jesus' words "This *is* [not "represents"] my body" continued to bother me. Scripturally speaking, it looked more and more like Jesus was not speaking symbolically, but sacramentally, when He said this, particularly in light of the fact that He did not say, "This bread is a symbol of my flesh" nor "This bread is my teaching" nor "This bread is my spirit" but "This bread *is my flesh*, which I will give for the life of the world" (John 6:51 [NIV]). After all, the first people to interpret these words literally were standing right next to Him. As John 6:60 tells us, "Many of his disciples, when they heard it, said, 'This is a hard saying; who can listen to it?'" In other words, they responded exactly the way I had been taught to respond as a Protestant: "Hey! This is far-fetched. This is a difficult statement. Must be the product of Dark Ages thinking." Scripture goes on to say that many people left Jesus after He said this. What Scripture does *not* say is that Jesus ran after them calling, "Hey guys! Time out! Metaphor! Metaphor! I was just speaking *symbolically*. Relax! Don't take me so literally!" And that, I was coming to believe, is because Jesus meant exactly what He said. The harder I pushed to try to keep these words "merely symbolic" the harder Jesus and the apostles began to push back, insisting, in Paul's words, "The cup of blessing which we bless, is it not a *participation* in the blood of Christ? The bread which we break, is it not a *participation* in the body of Christ?" (1 Corinthians 10:16). In fact, Paul was so insistent on what looked for all the world like the actual sacramental presence of Christ in Communion that he sternly warned the Corinthians, "Whoever, therefore, eats the bread or drinks the cup of the Lord in an unworthy manner will be guilty of profaning the body and blood of the Lord" (1 Corinthians 11:27). Strong words for a "mere symbol." And pretty confusing ones as well if you are trying to get across the idea that Eucharist merely "represents" Jesus. It would imply that Christ's hand-picked apostles were not just bad teachers, but specially and spectacularly inept ones.

In fact, their ineptitude would have to be something almost unique in history to convince so many of their disciples so thoroughly of something so far from what they "really meant" to say. For as I continued studying the Church that came after the apostles, I discovered something shocking: nobody — absolutely nobody — spoke of the Eucharist as being a "mere symbol" for the first thousand years of the Church! To be sure, they spoke of it as symbolic, just as they spoke of Jesus as a man. But, just as they never spoke of Jesus as being *only* a man, so they never spoke of Eucharist as being *only* a symbol. Rather, the uniform belief of the Church following the apostles for a thousand years was pretty well summed up by Ignatius of Antioch (who was a disciple of the Apostle John and wrote around 107 AD). He said, passing on what he (and all the other early Christians who taught about the Eucharist) taught was the teaching of the apostles, that "The Eucharist is the Flesh of our Savior Jesus Christ, Flesh which suffered for our sins and which the Father, in His goodness, raised up again."[1] This was the Faith of the Church taught by the apostles and it wasn't even questioned for another thousand years. In fact, it was the idea of the Eucharist as a *mere symbol*, and not the idea of it as the actual Body and Blood of Jesus, that was the product of "Dark Ages thinking."

That presented a further problem to me. If the Eucharist was really Jesus Christ Himself, really present in a sacramental way and not merely a symbol of Him, then it was, as Paul said, a *participation* in His once-for-all sacrifice. And if it was a participation in His sacrifice, then the one who offered it was participating in Christ's *priesthood* in a special way like the Levites (who had a special priesthood in contrast to the common priesthood of Israel). My initial, hopeful thought was that the New Testament got rid of this special priesthood. But the more I studied Scripture, the more doubtful this looked. For when Peter said (1 Peter 2:9), "You are a chosen race, a royal priesthood, a holy nation, God's own people," he wasn't saying anything *new*. He was simply quoting Exodus 19:5–6. He wasn't saying, "In the Old Covenant only Levites were priests but now everyone is a priest," for the very simple reason that under the Old Covenant Levites were not the only priests. Rather, they had a special, consecrated priesthood in contrast to the common priesthood in which all Israel shared. What if it was the same under the New Covenant?

The more I studied, the more it looked as though this was the case. Under the Old Covenant, you entered the common priesthood by virtue of your circumcision. Under the New Covenant, you entered it by virtue of baptism. But merely being circumcised did not make you a Levit-

---

[1] Ignatius, *Letter to the Smyrnaeans*, 7, 1.

ical priest. Nor could you claim the Levitical priesthood for yourself even if you were a Levite. Rather, as Hebrews 5:4 points out, "One does not take the honor upon himself, but he is called by God just as Aaron was." Under the Old Covenant, "called by God" did not mean "having a special warm feeling in your heart that assures you that you are a Levitical priest." It meant going through a formal process of ordination to the priesthood that was public and performed by one who was himself already a priest in the line of Aaron. Trying to do independent jazz riffs on this very orderly process of priestly succession by, say, offering unauthorized sacrifices (as Nadab and Abihu did [Leviticus 10:1–3]) received stern judgment in no uncertain terms.

And the New Testament, though it instituted a new and final sacrifice in Christ, did not seem to have anything to say against this basic process of orderly succession. "John Doe" Christian could not simply grab a piece of bread and cup of wine and declare it to be the Body and Blood of Christ. On the contrary, Justin Martyr (writing circa 150 AD) summed up early Christian teaching on the subject when he said:

> The apostles, in the Memoirs which they produced, which are called gospels, have thus passed on that which was enjoined upon them: that Jesus took bread and, having given thanks, said, "Do this in remembrance of me; this is my body." And in like manner, taking the cup, and having given thanks, he said, "This is my blood." *And he imparted this to them only.*[2]

In other words, the whole of the early Church insisted that it was taught by the apostles that not all Christians

---

[2] Justin Martyr, *First Apology*, 66, emphasis added.

could consecrate the sacrament. Only apostles and those whom the apostles designated (Acts 14:23), such as Timothy and Titus and those such successors themselves designated (Titus 1:5), could do so. In fact, Justin Martyr himself was not a successor to the apostles and, therefore, only received the Eucharist; he did not consecrate it.

Which meant I had yet another problem. As an independent pastor, not only did not I (nor anyone else in my church) have any real authority (as Timothy, for instance, received from Paul) to "charge certain persons not to teach any different doctrine" (1 Timothy 1:3), I also had no particular reason for thinking I could consecrate communion just because I had stuck the word "pastor" in front of my name. I was earnest, I was sincere, I was reverent. I believed (and still believe) that God blessed our celebration of communion as He blesses any gesture of love offered to Him. But that doesn't mean sincerity equals apostolic authority. I no more had the authority that Timothy enjoyed from Paul than I had the power to "command and teach" authoritatively (1 Timothy 4:11).

All of this made me more uncertain than ever and none of it was helped as I continued my studies of Scripture and the early Church Fathers. For as I did, I became more and more interested in the ancient Jewish and early Church concept of "the word of God." As I soon discovered in my studies of Jewish roots, Jews believed that God's word, the Torah, came to Moses in both written form — the five books of Moses — *and* in unwritten form, later to be written down as the Talmud.[3]

Of course, many people will say at this point, "But the

---

[3] Hayim Halevy Donin, *To Be a Jew: A Guide to Jewish Observance in Contemporary Life* (New York: Basic Books, 1991), pp. 24–25.

Jews were just wrong to think this way. After all, Jesus condemned all tradition when He rebuked the Pharisees saying, 'You leave the commandment of God, and hold fast the tradition of men' (Mark 7:8)." But this is to misread Jesus. For Jesus did not condemn *all* tradition; He condemned confusing the traditions of men with the Tradition of God. How do we know? Because Jesus Himself teaches from both the written Torah *and* the unwritten Torah, like all good rabbis. That is why Jesus can refer to the teaching office in Israel by the title "Moses' Seat" even though that title exists nowhere in the Old Testament and is found only in Jewish tradition. It is also why Jesus makes free use of pre-existing stories and parables in Jewish tradition and adapts them to his own purposes (such as the parable of the Good Samaritan in Luke 10, which is adapted from a rabbinic tale later preserved in the Tosefta [Yom HaKipurim 1:12]). In short, Jesus honors the concept of the unwritten Torah. *He distinguishes, not between Tradition and Scripture, but between human tradition and that Tradition handed down to us from God.* Jesus' criticism of the scribes and Pharisees in Mark 7:13, "that you have invalidated the word of God by your tradition," is not a blanket condemnation of all tradition, but rather a correction regarding a tradition of man (called *corban*) that had choked the power of the word of God. According to this tradition, a son could take money which should have gone for the care of his parents and consider it as *corban*, a gift devoted to God. Once money was considered *corban* the son did not necessarily have to give the money to the Temple and could use the money for himself. By doing this he could legally exclude his parents from receiving the gift and thus shirk his responsibility to care for them as the commandment to honor one's father and mother requires of him. Wouldn't you condemn a tradition like that? Joseph Cardinal Ratzinger points out that the "traditions were criticized in order that genuine tradition might be revealed."[4] This view is consistent in apostolic teaching as well. That is why St. Paul tells the Thessalonians, "Stand firm and hold to the traditions which you were taught by us, either by word of mouth or by letter" (2 Thessalonians 2:15). The traditions to which St. Paul refers are known as apostolic Tradition. There is a distinction between the traditions of the Church (sometimes referred to as small 't' traditions) and the apostolic Tradition (referred to as big 'T' traditions). When the Church speaks of apostolic Tradition, she is not speaking of the disciplinary, liturgical, or devotional traditions developed in the local churches over the years. These traditions can be modified or entirely dropped under the guidance of the Magisterium. Apostolic Tradition, however, comes to us from the apostles as they received it from Jesus. They received this from His teaching, from His example, and from what the Holy Spirit revealed to them. It is this apostolic Tradition that is referred to when the Catholic Church speaks of Scripture and Tradition making up the deposit of faith. From her inception, the Church understood that she was to share the *full* deposit of faith, written and unwritten.

The problem was that, at NCF, I was living in a system that only respected the Bible as the word of God and did not really revere Tradition in either the Jewish or early Church way. To be sure, tradition (especially Jewish tradition) colored what we did, but we did not really think of it (and still less of early Christian tradition) as funda-

---

[4] *Principles of Catholic Theology* (San Francisco: Ignatius Press, 1987), p. 95.

mentally altering any belief that "Scripture alone is the sole source of revelation." Nor did we ever resolve the fact that there was no apostolic authority at work to get us past the "he saith/she saith" dilemma in any serious dispute about Scripture, tradition, or how to run the church on a practical day-to-day basis. I began to see with greater and greater clarity the irony of our attempt to build a "New Testament church" that, however connected we were to Jewish roots, was almost entirely unconnected to *Christian* roots. We were completely unfamiliar with any other denomination, any other independent church, and any church that had existed for the past 2,000 years. In fact, we didn't even know what the rest of the believing church *believed*. It looked more and more odd to me that we should have, as we did, this distinctly inflated sense that we were The Church that God was using and speaking to as if we were the only one that existed. This seemed to me to be giving us a bit more credit than we deserved. We'd set out to build the new Jerusalem; we'd ended up with a badly wounded little church in Ohio and a pastor who wasn't sure what he believed, why he believed it, and whether he had the authority to be a pastor at all. So finally, after a great deal of anguished thought about this I came to the conclusion that I wanted to be a part of the Charismatic Episcopal Church.

Not surprisingly, rumor soon got out that I was thinking about all this. I talked to the elders at NCF about it and they told me I could become, if I wanted, a Charismatic Episcopal priest and still pastor NCF, but that the church did not want to convert with me. This somewhat fuzzy arrangement seemed okay to me at the time, but then again I was pretty tentative in my thinking too. I was still hoping to effect some compromise between my leanings toward the Charismatic Episcopal Church and my duty to NCF.

So I put out feelers to Deacon Bane about all this stuff and he soon asked me to come to Kansas City to meet with his bishop about the possibility of coming into the Charismatic Episcopal Church. When his call came, I thought, "Wow!" but then I developed cold feet. Undecided, I told him, "Let me think about it."

A little later that afternoon, he called me back and said, "I've just got this sense that you're supposed to come out here and that God is going to do something in your life." When he said that, it was like something clicked inside me. Somehow, I knew he was right. God *was* about to do something in my life.

So Emily and I decided to fly out to Kansas City. I was thinking absolutely nothing about the Catholic Church. My mind was entirely on the Episcopal church. And that, I thought, was the way it always would be.

Bait and Switch

We met with Episcopal Bishop Randolph Sly and things went extremely well. I thought for certain, "This is everything I've been studying *toward*!" It looked more and more like the answer to the hunger in my heart and everything that God's Providence had put in my path for the past decade or more. Here was liturgy, sacramentality, form, and leadership.

The church in Kansas City was composed of a large number of former Catholics as well as Episcopalians and charismatics. The family we stayed with numbered among these former Catholics. They were so warm and so excited about their faith! They reminded me somehow of those early days in the charismatic movement. And when we went to liturgy, it was much the same. It was a high Episcopalian liturgy with all the beautiful gold vestments and majestic pomp, (held, of all places, in the gym of a public school) but the homily sounded like an Evangelical message and, when they elevated the Host, there was a period of prayer and praise in tongues and some absolutely beautiful worship of God. When it was all done, I felt more certain than ever that this was where I was going to go.

However, after the service was over, I walked over to the book table and saw this book entitled *Evangelical Is Not Enough* by Thomas Howard (brother of Elisabeth Eliot). I thought, "Wow!" The subtitle was *Worship of God in Liturgy and Sacrament*! So I picked up the book and thought, "This guy is singing my song too! Cool!" I looked at Emily and exclaimed, "This is what we've been talking about!" Emily was excited too because she had been feeling the same way and experiencing the same hunger and desire as me in all this. So I bought the book and started reading immediately. I was delighted that I found another person who was expounding on all the ideas that I had had. Later that day, we left Kansas City feeling positive about a move toward this denomination.

On the plane home I read Howard's book straight through. I was so excited that I kept nudging Emily and saying, "You've gotta listen to this! You've gotta listen to this! This guy's saying exactly everything I've been going through! Everything!" This excitement built and built throughout the flight until I came to the very end and my eyes fell on Howard's postscript:

> All of the foregoing was written during 1984 and the book was first published in that year. At the Easter Vigil in 1985, I was received into the Roman Catholic Church.[1]

I just about swallowed my bag of peanuts! "How did he do *that*?" I was stumped. I couldn't figure it out. This guy was saying the exact things that were going on in my life and he converted to the *Catholic Church*? He was playing my tune until he did that.

And that really *really* bothered me.

I thought about it for a long while. I had been so excited about the things that he was saying about liturgy, sacrament, sacred space, sacred time, the Incarnation and Resurrection and so forth. And now, here he was, no longer enjoying that with the Episcopal denomination! It irked

---

[1] Thomas Howard, *Evangelical Is Not Enough* (San Francisco: Ignatius, 1984), p. 157.

me because his journey led him, not just to a different church, but to the Church I had left! How could his con-clusion lead back to where I began? How could *that* be? How *could* it end up back there? I felt robbed! I wanted to be Episcopalian! I had gone to the conference thinking God was leading me to be Episcopalian! And now this! It was bait and switch!

But whatever my assumptions about how things were supposed to go, reality was beginning to act as though it had other plans and dropped little hints at me. The Joneses and the Xenia faction elders, after insisting they had not been planning a split, proceeded to announce that NCF was splitting in early 1994. The portion of the church that stayed with me decided to move our meeting place to Day-ton. So we began checking out the Bergamo Retreat Center as a possible new facility. It was a Catholic retreat center. As we went to look at the building, we happened to come in shortly after Mass, and the residue of incense still hung in the air. When I smelled that, it took me right back to my youth and grabbed me in a powerful way.

The possibility "Catholic" flickered through my mind for a millisecond.

But I thrust it away. After all, I was a pastor — a mar-ried pastor. What place was there for me in the Catholic Church with a resume like mine? How would I survive fi-nancially? My wife and child had to eat after all. The Epis-copalians, with their married priests, seemed much more reasonable on that score.

But still, Howard's book nagged at me. I wanted to find some way to argue with him that I could just remain Epis-copalian (as he should have done) and not go to the ex-treme of becoming Catholic. So I looked through the yel-low pages and (finding nothing about an Episcopal book store) I decided I would go to the Catholic book store and see if they had anything on the Episcopal church (it didn't yet occur to me to go to a Catholic bookstore to find out if they had anything on the *Catholic* Church). I wanted Episcopalian information on liturgy, church history, and sacraments to counter Howard's devastating impact. But that meant venturing into dangerous territory to find it. So I steeled myself, drove a mile from home to downtown Centerville, Ohio, and approached the front door of St. Mark's Catholic Bookstore. I paused, looked over both my shoulders, peered up and down the street to make sure no one saw me, and made a dash inside.

I found myself in a little shop stuffed with statues, holy water fonts, rosaries, icons, plaques of the Sacred Heart and Mary and various saints. I stood there, thinking to myself, "Oh wow!" It had been so long since I'd been in this sort of environment. For a Minnesota boy like me, it felt so foreign. Yet, in another way, something deep within me resonated with it all. It was like that moment in the Bergamo Retreat Center all over again. I felt as though I was hanging in space between two worlds. On the one hand, I was terribly worried about being seen by somebody. On the other hand, I wanted to act like I knew what I was doing in this alien world. After standing there, dithering for a minute, I quickly went over to the books where I was more at home. Books I understood. And as I wandered around I eventually found this book called *Catholicism and Fundamentalism* by Karl Keating. I'd never heard of him before, but as I looked through it I thought, "This is pretty interesting!" Then I opened a copy of the *Catechism of the Catholic Church*. My eyes fell on paragraph 133 which said, "The Church 'forcefully and specifically exhorts all the Christian faithful . . . to learn "the surpass-

ing knowledge of Jesus Christ," by frequent reading of the
divine Scriptures. "Ignorance of the Scriptures is ignorance
of Christ."'" I was a bit confused. I had never heard this
coming from Catholics. So I bought Keating's book and
the *Catechism* and took them home.

After this, curious things started to happen to me. I
started, on my own, studying the Catholic Church. After
reading Howard's and Keating's books and studying the
Church Fathers, it was like a little flame was kindled inside
of me and the hunger became sharper. It was a hunger,
not only for truth, but most especially for the Eucharist.
It was so overwhelming and so acute that I found myself
gripped with the thought, "I have *got* to go to Mass! Even
though I can't receive the Eucharist, I have to go!"

So I went to a Saturday evening Mass at a parish in
Centerville, Ohio. Once there, I snuck in incognito (shades
and all) and ducked down into a pew in the very back of
the church, just to be there. Even so, as I looked around
I realized to my horror that the congregation was dotted
with face after face of persons who I recognized from the
community who, if they glanced my way, would recognize
me too! So I laid low in the back pew in terror of being
seen. Yet at the same time, I spent the whole liturgy trying
to master myself because I was on the verge of bursting
into tears, so sharp was my hunger for what I now knew
to be the Body and Blood of Christ. I remember, at one
point, feeling the temptation to stand up as people were
approaching the altar and shout, "Do you people realize
what you're receiving?!" For the first time in my life, the
full enormity of what was present on the altar was de-
scending on me with overwhelming force and yet with the
tenderest love. But still, my fear of being seen — of being
discovered — kept me quiet.

This conflict between the overwhelming power of love that urged me on and the fear that held me back produced odd (and as I look back on it, funny) results. My house became a wilderness of books as I was swept up in a frenzy of study. I had dozens of books all laid out on the floor: books on Mary, the papacy, Purgatory, etc., along with the *Catechism of the Catholic Church* and the various writings of the Fathers and so forth. If you'd been a mouse in the corner in those days you would have seen me there on my hands and knees, poring over up to fifteen or twenty books and hopping from book to book as I chased down one idea after another. There were tapes, there were videos, there were resources of every size and shape. But whenever somebody came to our door, I had to scramble to gather all this up and hide it! I was petrified that somebody might see me reading *Catholic* things.

Yet despite my cowardice, God was gracious and continued to show me wonderful things through my studies. I felt like a man putting together a 3,000 piece jigsaw puzzle. As time went on, I began to realize that I had been led by the Holy Spirit to construct the borders of the puzzle. First, as a Protestant, He had shown me the border called "Sacred Scripture." I had learned it very well but then, as happens with jigsaw puzzles, my finger had followed the left edge up and up until suddenly it took a sharp right turn at Open Arms Church. There, the Holy Spirit had begun to show me the top edge of the puzzle: the edge called "Sacred Tradition." That was why the Jewish roots movement had been so important and that, in turn, had led me to study the concept of the word of God and the way in which Tradition affected how we read Scripture as well. This in turn led to another sharp turn down the right edge of the puzzle, the border called "Sacramentality" and all the implications which sprang from the Incarnation of Jesus Christ and His Revelation to and through His Church. And this, in turn, led to the bottom edge of the puzzle: "Authority of the Church."

I now felt very certain of two things: first, that it was indeed the Holy Spirit Who had shown me these four edges of the jigsaw puzzle and second, that these four edges *framed* whatever picture was supposed to be in the middle of the puzzle. I was acutely conscious at the time that God was wooing me through this journey of discovery. But I was not at all sure initially what I was going to discover or what that jigsaw puzzle picture would turn out to be. Was it the Episcopal church? Orthodoxy? The Catholic Church? I had to know.

Increasingly, I began to study the early Church Fathers, those great Christian writers and thinkers who lived from the first to the eighth centuries. In addition, I started reading some of Luther and Calvin, as well as the documents of various Church councils. All the while, of course, I continued to study the Jewish roots materials as well.

By mid-1994, I was talking to Emily about the Catholic Church and was reading the *Catechism* and *Catholic and Christian* by Dr. Alan Schreck, a gift from my mother. I was reading it steadily and, as with Howard's book, exclaiming to Emily, "Listen to this! Listen to this! Listen to what this guy said! Listen to what that guy said!" What kept exciting me was the way in which so much of the teaching of the Catholic Church fit together — just like the pieces of the jigsaw puzzle. All that was so exciting about the Convergence Movement was present — from ancient times — in the Catholic Church. The hallowing of time in the liturgical year; the blessing of ritual, sign, and symbol; the raising of creation to participate in sacramentality: all this the Episcopal church had inherited from the Catholic Church. In addition, the problem of authority that had so plagued NCF was answered by the Catholic reality of apostolic succession. Priests derive their authority from bishops and bishops derive their authority from bishops before them in a line of succession going all the way back to the apostles. Catholics did not have to make things up as they went along. I kept marveling to Emily, "Everything hangs together! It just all hangs together so well!"

In a strange and paradoxical way, this was true even of the things that my Protestant heritage regarded as difficult. For example, Mary. Mary, in fact, began as a double difficulty for me because the Church's doctrine of her perpetual virginity appeared to me to contradict what I had learned in the Jewish roots movement. In Judaism, sex is emphatically good. In fact, according to Jewish tradition, regular sexual relations with one's spouse were commanded. It was so important that there were detailed regulations one followed according to one's state in life. If you were a camel herder and were often required to be away from home, tradition relaxed the demand for frequent relations with your wife. If you were a scholar, tradition strictly bound you to much more frequent relations with her. All of this, of course, posed a problem for me in that it made it difficult to believe that the Catholic picture of Mary and Joseph was a picture easily reconcilable with a good Jewish couple.

But as I began to study the Church's Tradition more deeply and to read the New Testament in light of it, I began to see that it was not a question of sex being denigrated and virginity being opposed to it, but of sex and marriage being good and virginity being better. It was, after all, Jesus who praised those who made themselves "eunuchs for the sake of the kingdom of heaven" (Matthew 19:12). And,

He Himself — a man emphatically expected, at His age, to be married and have children — chose the way of virginity in transcendence of the expectation of Jewish tradition. Likewise, Paul chose the way of virginity and praised it highly as well (1 Corinthians 7). And so the Church had done through the ages, never denigrating marriage (in fact, regarding it as a sacrament), but still exalting virginity. I began to realize that the Catholic Church's picture of Mary "fit" the revelation in Christ better than Jewish tradition did. Especially since, when I began to really look at the evidence, it became apparent that there was no solid biblical evidence that Mary had other children and quite a bit of evidence that she did indeed remain a virgin.

The two bits of evidence that seemed the most solid in favor of Mary's having other children were the biblical references to Jesus' "brothers and sisters" and Matthew's comment that Joseph "knew her not until she had borne a son" (Matthew 1:25). However, as I studied, I found that solidity melting away. In the first place, my Jewish roots studies had shown me that like anyone else, biblical writers did not stop thinking according to their native language any more than native English speakers do when they smuggle English ideas into Japanese when attempting to speak it. And so, just as English speakers say *"aisu kurimu"* when speaking of "ice cream" in Japanese, so ancient native speakers of Hebrew often tended to use "brother" or "sister" as a kind of slang term to refer to more distant relatives such as cousins and saw no reason to stop the practice when they happened to be writing in Greek. This being so, it became very difficult to tell whether the Gospels were referring to siblings or cousins of Jesus when they spoke of His "brothers." The difficulty of this is highlighted by a comparison of Galatians, James, and Jude. In Galatians, Paul calls James "the Lord's brother" (Galatians 1:19). James, however, calls himself only a "servant of the Lord Jesus Christ" not His brother (James 1:1). Likewise, Jude, in turn, refers to himself as "a servant of the Lord Jesus Christ and brother of James" but not of Jesus (Jude 1). Jude looks a great deal as though he considers James his sibling, but not Jesus. In other words, it begins to look very much as though James and Jude are siblings to one another and cousins of Jesus.

In addition, I also found that Matthew's remark about Joseph having no relations with Mary "until she had borne a son" was not as cut and dried as it seemed. And it was not Catholic theologians, but Protestant reformers who showed me this. Luther, Calvin, and Zwingli (not to mention Wesley), all insisted that her perpetual virginity was biblical teaching and that Matthew was implying absolutely nothing about Mary having relations with Joseph after the birth of Christ. And the more I looked at that, the more sense it made. Mark Shea, Catholic apologist and friend, encapsulates this concept nicely in his recent book:

> The passage in Matthew which says Joseph "had no union with her until she gave birth to a son" (Matthew 1:25) does not necessarily imply anything about Mary's subsequent relationship with Joseph since the word "until" is ambiguous. This is seen, for instance, in Deuteronomy 1:31, where Moses tells Israel that "the LORD your God carried you, as a father carries his son, all the way you went *until* you reached this place." Moses does not mean that God stopped carrying Israel once they reached Canaan, for he has just finished saying God will continue to fight for them just as He always has. Likewise, in Deuteronomy 9:7 Moses tells Israel, "From the day you left Egypt *until* you arrived here, you have been rebellious against the LORD." Moses is not saying that Israel, once they arrived at the border

of Canaan, ceased being rebellious. Similarly, when Luke
tells us that John the Baptist "lived in the desert *until*
he appeared publicly to Israel" (Luke 1:80), he does not
mean to imply that John stopped living in the desert after
he began his public ministry. For as the Baptist himself
says (and Luke records) John's ministry was precisely "a
voice of one calling in the desert" (Luke 3:4). In the same
way then, Matthew is not implying that Mary, once she
brought forth Jesus, ceased being a virgin. He is simply
saying that she conceived Him in virginity and making
no implications whatever about any post-partum sexual
relations between Mary and Joseph. Therefore, Scripture
does not forbid the Catholic understanding of Mary's virginity.[2]

More than this however, the biblical account of the virgin birth not only did not support my traditional Protestant assumption that Mary had other children, it raised real
doubts about it. Here's why:

Joseph, upon finding Mary was "with child of the Holy
Spirit" was "resolved to send her away quietly" (Matthew
1:18–19). There are two views of the actions of St. Joseph
in Matthew 1. The first (which I had always assumed to
be the only one) may be called the Suspicion Theory. This
view, which is most common among moderns, is that Joseph
disbelieved Mary, suspected her of adultery, and contem-
plated divorcing her in accord with Deuteronomy 24:1–4.
The theory holds that St. Joseph tried to do this secretly to
avoid subjecting Mary to the death penalty (Deuteronomy
22:23–24). The difficulty with this theory is that the "righ-

---

[2] Mark P. Shea, "What Is the Relationship Between Scripture and
Tradition?" in *Not by Scripture Alone: A Catholic Critique of the Protes-
tant Doctrine of Sola Scriptura*, Robert A. Sungenis, ed. (Santa Barbara:
Queenship, 1997), pp. 203–204.

teousness" of Joseph's character is hard to reconcile with a willingness to simply ignore part of the Deuteronomic code. Selective obedience to the law of God does not square well with righteousness.

The early Fathers thought the same way, and as I studied I found, in fact, that many of them (for example, St. Jerome, the premier Scripture scholar of antiquity) held a very different theory concerning St. Joseph's actions — a theory that bears serious reconsideration. This theory may be called the Reverence Theory. It holds that Joseph *believed* Mary when she told him she was "with child of the Holy Spirit" and that, precisely because he was a righteous man, he recognized his own unworthiness before God to be the husband of such a woman chosen for such an honor.

Consider the psychological merits of this reading of Matthew and Luke by putting yourself in Joseph's shoes. You are a pious first century Jew who believes in angels. A godly woman you have known for years and whom you love and know to be absolutely trustworthy and not given to flakiness tells you she received a visitation from an angel last night when she was at prayer. She is not given to hysteria or tall tales and she is dead serious. She tells you the angel said she would bear a son by the Holy Spirit. She says the angel told her that her aged cousin is pregnant too. A little time passes and then you find out the cousin *is* pregnant despite her advanced age. As weeks and months roll on, you find your beloved is indeed pregnant, too. She looks at you with absolutely honest eyes and says, "Don't you remember when I told you about the angel and his message?" Do you believe her? I think I would. I know I would believe Emily under similar circumstances. And I know how unworthy I felt to be Emily's husband. So, would I feel more or less unworthy of Emily if I discovered

she was pregnant of the Holy Spirit? That's not too hard
to figure out.

Read in this way, the biblical text makes more sense than
it does when read through the lens of the Suspicion Theory. First, Joseph's resolve to be secretive is then seen as
a reverent and discreet attempt to keep secret what God
has chosen to keep secret. Second, it makes sense of the
angel's urging that Joseph not "fear" to take Mary as his
wife. Finally, it explains why the angel is careful to address
Joseph as "son of David": he is being reminded the Messiah is to come through the line of David and that the role
has been appointed for him by God, despite his feelings of
unworthiness.

Further, it makes sense of something that no one seems
to notice in all the haggling about the meaning of the
word "until" in Matthew 1:25. Namely, why did Joseph
have no relations with Mary *before* she gave birth? After all, Joseph, having taken Mary into his home, had full
conjugal rights and most married couples do not suspend
these rights for the entire duration of a pregnancy. Yet for
some strange reason Joseph opted to do just this. Why?
The puzzle piece that fits best here is the Catholic doctrine
of the perpetual virginity of Mary. Joseph did not exercise
his conjugal rights *before* the birth of Jesus for the same
reason he did not exercise them *after* the birth of Jesus:
because he regarded Mary as a consecrated virgin and a
kind of "second Ark of the Covenant." It was not a difficult connection for him to make, especially since the angel Gabriel had already suggested the connection when he
said, "The Holy Spirit will come upon you, and power of
the Most High will overshadow you" (Luke 1:35) just as
the Shekinah glory had overshadowed the Tabernacle and
the Ark of the Covenant in the Old Testament (Numbers

9:15). Nor did the connection escape the attention of the early Church. Certainly the early Church Fathers saw the connection. In the old ark resided the word of God written on two stone tablets; in Mary, the new ark, resides the Word of God who became flesh. In the ark we see manna; the new ark contained the living bread which came down from Heaven. In the old ark resided the rod of Aaron, the high priest; in Mary resided the eternal high priest, Jesus. That is why John, in his Revelation, shows us first the Ark of the Covenant (Revelation 11:19) and then immediately presents an image of a woman clothed with the sun who gives birth to a "male child, who ruled the nations with an iron scepter" (Revelation 12:5). Again, in the words of Mark Shea:

> The connection between Mary and the Ark, once it is made, is hard not to see. Knowing the identity of Mary's "male child," it would be an easy mental connection for any pious Jew to immediately think of her as a kind of second Ark.
>
> Well, Joseph of Nazareth *was* a pious Jew. And, after his dream (Matthew 1:23) he *did* know the identity of Mary's "male child." He also knew, as a Jew steeped in the Old Testament, what happens to people who touch the Ark without authorization (2 Samuel 6:6–8). So it becomes very psychologically probable that Joseph, knowing what he knew, also would have chosen celibacy in this rather unusual situation.[3]

To my amazement then, this Catholic doctrine "fit the puzzle" in a surprising and satisfying way. It explained

---

[3] Shea, "What is the Relationship Between Scripture and Tradition?" in *Not by Scripture Alone: A Catholic Critique of the Protestant Doctrine of Sola Scriptura*, p. 207.

why Jesus gave Mary to John and not to His siblings as He hung upon the cross: He had no siblings. It explained why Mary — a betrothed woman — expressed surprise at the prospect that she would have children (a surprise, when you think about it, that is only explicable if she had already made a private vow of virginity). It fit the pattern established by our Lord Himself in His own virginity. It was psychologically probable for Joseph. And it makes sense in the context of the whole biblical and patristic praise of virginity. Once again, it all hung together.

It was the same with another difficulty: the history of the papacy. It's no secret that there have been some pretty bad popes in the past and that bothered me. But, again, as I began to look at Scripture it became increasingly apparent to me that Catholic teaching about the office of the pope in fact followed the biblical pattern, even when the pope was a stinker. In the Old Testament, for example, many of the great leaders God used had been guilty of crimes every bit as heinous as any bad pope. Moses had killed a man. Paul had been part of the mob that stoned Stephen to death. King David was a murderer and an adulterer. Yet in every case, including that of King David, when God's leaders failed, God either restored them or brought in new leaders to fill the office, but He never simply swept the office out of existence. Under the old covenant, King Saul was replaced by David and King David was chastised for his sin, but the office of King was not simply annihilated. In the same way, even the ultimate sin of betraying the Son of God did not mean that Judas' office of apostle was obliterated by God. Yes, Judas personally lost his place as an apostle. But significantly, the Church considered his office still valid. That is why, after Pentecost, they chose Matthias to replace Judas with the words, "His office let another take" (Acts 1:20).

God, in short, never ripped down the whole program and started again from scratch — even with Judas. How much less then was I to suppose He had done so with the office of the man to whom He said, "You are Peter, and on this rock I will build my church, and the powers of death shall not prevail against it" (Matthew 16:18). And where else was that office — that sign of the unity that I so much longed for and for which Jesus prayed in John 17 — than in the man universally acknowledged in the ancient Church as the successor of Peter: the Pope? It was here, more than anywhere else, that both the Episcopal and Orthodox paths, for all their glories, simply did not seem to me to hold to the fulness of the biblical picture. So in an odd way, this difficulty too had the strange effect of nudging me closer to the Catholic Church.

As the months rolled on, I continued to labor away at that 3,000 piece jigsaw puzzle. The borders of Scripture, Tradition, Church authority, and the Sacraments were firmly in place. Bit by bit, the different expressions of doctrine within the Church kept fitting into their place. Part of the process was intellectual: just figuring out what the Church taught and whether it made rational sense. But another part of the process was deeply intuitive as well, which some people may view as a weakness. I think instead that I was approaching the Gospel with all of me and not just my head. And I will be honest, I found the Catholic understanding of the Gospel as deeply satisfying to my emotions as it was to my mind. There was, I will make no pretense about it, a sense of being emotionally drawn back to the faith that I knew as a child. There was the comfort of being loved by the clergy, by *fathers,* especially that Holy Father, the Pope. There were the images, the smells, the sounds, the whole incarnational reality for which my studies of Jewish roots had prepared me. The theology made rational sense, but the truth that was sketched by the theology was no mere sketch itself. It *was* reality and it sang to my very bones.

So it is not strange to me, though it is still beautiful and wonderful, that one evening after I had taken out the garbage, I found myself standing behind our apartment building, looking up at the stars and thinking, "I want to sign myself with the Sign of the Cross." I wanted to do it just to see what it felt like. I had done it for years as a child without thinking and then, for the past decade or so, I had not done it at all. So, again cautiously looking around to make sure there were no witnesses, I made the Sign of the Cross and said quietly, "In the name of the Father, and of the Son, and of the Holy Spirit."

The moment I did it, tears started rolling down my cheeks. I felt, "I'm coming home. I need to come home." There was something about signing myself, something sacramental, something that transcended words, that spoke to me in a way far more complete than mere rationalism or theology could speak. It wasn't that the Catholic Faith was irrational or anti-theological. It was rather that the Catholic Faith was *bigger* than rationalism. And so, when I made the Sign of the Cross I knew down to the very core of my being that something had *happened*. I had changed even more and some identification with Jesus had taken place that I had not known in years.

I stood out there thinking, "This is crazy! I come outside, where nobody can see me, to *practice* the Sign of the Cross!" But there it was. The experience was so powerful that it prompted me to do something else I had not done in ages: and that was to pray the "Our Father." It was funny. As a Protestant, I had preached about, thought about, and taught about the "Our Father." But seldom had I or any of the churches I was affiliated with actually prayed it. Now I was praying it in earnest. And when I finished I made the Sign of the Cross again.

It felt exactly right, like putting on a pair of wonderful gloves or old shoes that were well broken in.

Of course, try as I might to be discreet, my studies were nonetheless having an effect on my ministry. In fact, I had begun preaching from the *Catechism* in our Sunday morning services (while quietly neglecting to mention to my congregation where I was getting my stuff). All my discoveries about the concept of the Word of God, about sign, symbol, and sacrament, about tradition and the authority of the Church were percolating into my sermons. I taught on the "Our Father" and used material from Catholic sources. People were coming up to me after church saying, "Whoa! That's great stuff!" Emily, however, for all her enthusiasm about the Convergence Movement, was suddenly very turned off to the Catholic Church with a stiffness that was very unlike her. I vividly remember her saying, "I am *not* going to be Catholic *and our daughter's not going to be.*" It was understandable. Later she told me, "I didn't know what becoming Catholic would entail, so out of my lack of understanding I resisted what you were trying to tell me." Consequently, she ignored the books I recommended she read and avoided discussion of the subject. However, she did quietly begin to use a Catholic prayer book I had acquired.

Meanwhile, my interest only deepened, though not without rough patches, as the following story will tell.

Sometime during this period, I had heard of some network on cable television that appeared to be "all Catholic, all the time." It featured some nun but I didn't know anything else about it. That made me curious, so shortly before Christmas 1994, I called the cable company to ask, "Do you guys carry that Catholic television station with the nun?" They said, "You mean EWTN. The answer is no, we don't carry it. But we're gonna be getting it sometime in the next year."

I said, "Oh. Okay."

Now at the same time as this burgeoning interest in the Church, something else was happening. I was starting to develop a little idol in my life: mutual funds and investing. As with most idols, this one was conceived in my heart with something that appeared to be the best of intentions: the care of my family. As I mentioned above, being a Protestant pastor was hard enough. No pastor is particularly well-paid and a pastor of a relatively small independent congregation ripped apart by internal strife can generally count on an even less stable income. But a pastor who is in this situation *and* is seriously contemplating returning to the Catholic Church really has a small paycheck to look forward to if he follows where God is leading. So all the while I was struggling with my questions about the Catholic jigsaw puzzle, I was also struggling to figure out how we were going to survive financially when and if I completed the puzzle.

As it happened, one of the ministries I had developed as a pastor was centered around helping other people get out of debt and begin to invest for retirement and for college education for their children. So as my future became more and more precarious as a Protestant pastor, I became more and more interested (some might use the words "mildly obsessed") with a show on CNBC called *Your Portfolio*. And as I watched this show more and more, I became increasingly involved in strategizing about mutual funds and finance. It came to a point where I watched this show every night and only then would I study the Bible, prepare to preach, and continue my studies of the Catholic Church. Slowly but surely, investment, mutual funds — Mammon — was coming to rival my love for the things of God. And I knew it. But I excused myself by saying that I was tired and weary after twelve years of fighting and struggling with tight finances. In fact, during the middle of all of this I was actually offered an investment job with a firm in Daytona Beach, Florida. And I might have taken it — had not something happened.

In December 1994, we went home to Minneapolis for Christmas. Before we left, I set up the VCR to record *Your Portfolio* every single night so that when I came back I would not have missed a broadcast. When we returned from Christmas vacation, I was excited to watch my *Your Portfolio* tapes. I came in at 1:00 in the morning, dropped all the luggage right there in the living room, scurried over to the VCR, and hit "rewind." Emily and Carly were exhausted, but I zipped into the kitchen, poured a soft drink, came back, and hit "play."

It was a tape of a Catholic Mass.

I said, "What the heck is *this*?" I hit "forward" several times. Same thing. "Forward" some more.

"Mother Angelica"?

What is *this*?

I didn't know anything about EWTN other than the little bit somebody had told me that had inspired me to call the cable company that one time. And now I was kind of miffed. So I called the cable company the next day and said, "What's going on? What happened to CNBC and *Your Portfolio* on channel 27?"

They said, "Three or four days ago we changed the channels and now EWTN is on channel 27."

Boom! Just like that, it was like the Lord spoke to my heart and said, "I am replacing that idol with the direction

I am moving you in: the Catholic Church." I looked over at Emily and for both of us it was the eeriest moment. I could practically hear the theme to *Twilight Zone* playing and feel the hand of God on my shoulder. Stranger still (as later events would prove) I remember distinctly sensing inside that the Holy Spirit was telling me, "This is your future."

Not long after, something else happened: I rented a video about the Pope's 1993 World Youth Day visit to Denver and I was not prepared for how it would affect me emotionally. Every two years the Pope calls together the youth from around the world for the purpose of sharing the Gospel and imparting vision. World Youth Day provides a unique opportunity for young people to see the enormity and diversity of the Church.

I put that video on to watch it while Emily was fixing dinner. Mile High Stadium in Denver was packed to capacity with excited Catholics. The atmosphere was electric, like nothing I had ever seen. Suddenly, there was the whole spectacle of the Holy Father coming into the stadium with all of these youth weeping and waving their arms. One teenage girl in particular stood out. She looked directly into the camera and exuberantly mouthed the words, "He's so cool!" As I watched that, all of a sudden I started crying.

I thought to myself, "What is getting hold of me? I can't believe this!"

As I put the video on pause, Emily, who was setting the dining room table, noticed my tears. "What's gotten into you?" she asked with a puzzled expression.

I said, "You don't understand." Pointing to the screen, I said, "That's not Jimmy Swaggart, Jim Bakker, or Pat Robertson. That's *Papa*! That's my father!" Somehow it had become more and more clear to me that we didn't just need people who can administer or run a church or preach a sermon. I was coming face to face with my bankruptcy and I felt desperately alone. I needed someone, a flesh and blood person, who could *father* me, someone who could help me, guide me, and love me. I told Emily, "There are a lot of Catholics just like me who have left the Church and are not being fathered. They don't have priests and bishops who love them and care for them. They are alone." Pointing once again to the TV screen, I said, "All those people in Mile High Stadium, they are my family and I left them!"

At the same time, the puzzle of the Church did not go away because of these incidents. On the contrary, my curiosity was now sharper than ever. So I decided to do two things.

First, I called Catholic Answers, the ministry founded by Karl Keating, in order to bombard them with questions and seek a little companionship. I was graciously befriended by the kind, generous, and well-versed James Akin. We hit it off very well because he was interested in my background in the Jewish roots movement and I was interested in his phenomenal command of Catholic theology. James was very sweet. He would let me call him any time of the day or night and talk to him as long as I wanted to. I would fire questions at him left and right and, in fact, at the beginning of 1995 I flew out to San Diego to visit him, Karl, and Fr. Ray Ryland. All of them were wonderfully gracious people and were of enormous help to me.

The second thing I did was turn to the man who had lit the fuse. With the help of a mutual friend at Gordon College in Massachusetts, I managed to get Thomas Howard's number and resolved to call him. I was surprised to get hold of him right away.

Talking to Tom Howard on the phone was like talking to Shakespeare. He was very eloquent and articulate.

I stammered out, "Uh . . . uh, Mr. Howard? My name is Jeff Cavins. I'm a pastor out in Dayton, Ohio . . ." and I told him my story and how I had read his book. I told him, "I got to that point about the Catholic thing in the back of your book and I just need to know . . . why? What happened?" So he told me his story, about his hunger for the sacraments, his yearning for the ancient tradition and authority of the Church, and about his hunger for the truth. He described the way in which this had led him all the way back to Rome. When he finished, I said, "That's exactly what's been happening to me!" I started to choke up and I said, "I've gotta be honest with you. I'm scared. I think God's leading me in this direction and I don't know what to do! I'm a pastor! I've been a pastor for over ten years! I don't even know if I can *do* anything else! I'm a *professional*! If I come back to the Catholic Church it means giving up everything!"

He replied, "Jeffery, you need to talk to two fellows. One is Marcus Grodi and the other is Scott Hahn at Franciscan University." I had never heard of either one of them, but Tom told me that they had similar stories to mine in that they were both Protestant pastors who had converted to the Catholic Church.

So I called Scott Hahn and we hit it off immediately on the phone. I told him that Thomas Howard had given me his name. Within five minutes, we felt like brothers because there was that kindred spirit of both being Protestant ministers who had fallen in love with the Catholic Church. As we talked, I started to ask him some questions about how he dealt with the changes when he came into the Catholic Church, what was hard about it, and so forth. We also talked about the Jewish roots movement and then, suddenly, Scott stopped me in the middle of the conversation and said, "Jeff, I just have this funny feeling that you and I are going to be working closely together for a long time." I paused and literally looked at the phone thinking, "What?" It was a strange moment, but I didn't forget it.

In addition to talking with Scott, I called up Marcus Grodi and told him my story too. It turned out he was now running an organization called the *Coming Home Network* whose entire purpose was to act as a landing place and source of encouragement for Protestant ministers who were entering the Catholic Church. As we talked, Marcus finally asked, "Jeff, did you have a childhood pastor?"

I said, "Yeah. He was a guy called Fr. Paul Dudley." (He was not the priest who told me not to read the Gospel of John.)

Marcus said, "You mean Bishop Paul Dudley? He is a bishop now in South Dakota and he often comes out to visit the Franciscan University campus near where I live. You need to call him and talk."

When Worlds Collide Again

Fr. (now Bishop) Paul Dudley was the man who, when I was a young boy, was the example of Christ to me. He was simply a wonderful believer. When he had been our parish priest back in Bloomington, he was always walking around with a big smile, a gleam in his eye, and a really helpful word of encouragement. Everything about him spoke of hope and joy. He loved to be with the youth. He was the kind of man who would walk up, put his arm around your shoulder, and say warmly, "How are you doing, Jeff?" He always made you feel like a million bucks. I remembered, as a child, being impressed with him because during his homilies he always came out to the people to speak. He cared about us deeply. His Masses were always an exciting time for me. And even though I hadn't understood the message of Christ when I was a kid, I had always known that *this* man knew God. In fact, even after I'd left the Church I had thought about him off and on for years. So after my conversation with Marcus, I thought, "I *do* need to talk to Bishop Dudley."

And that made me very nervous.

I found his number in Sioux Falls, South Dakota, and I was shaking as I dialed the phone. I wanted to talk to him and tell him that I was drawn to the Church, but didn't know what to do. I reached his secretary and asked, "Is Bishop Dudley there?" She said, "Just a moment," and all of a sudden that familiar boyhood voice came on the line.

"This is Bishop Dudley."

That voice really hit me and I said, "Bishop, this is Jeff Cavins."

"Jeff Cavins. . . . Is your father Robert Cavins?" he asked.

I said, "Yeah!" I hadn't seen Bishop Dudley since I was fourteen years old.

He said, "Jeff! How are you doing?"

I said, "er . . . fine. Ummm . . . well . . . there is one problem. I'm a Protestant pastor."

"A pastor . . . How did that happen?" he asked.

So I began to explain to him how it all happened. He was so patient. He listened to me, and at the end of the conversation I became really choked up and said, "Bishop, I want to come home. But I don't know what to do. Frankly, I'm scared. And I don't know what to say to my parents because it would be like admitting they were right all that time."

He said, "Jeff, can you come out to Sioux Falls and spend a couple of days with me?"

I said, "Yes."

As a boy growing up, I was in awe of bishops. And since then I had not racked up a good record with bishops. Now here's a bishop inviting me to stay with him!

So I flew out to Sioux Falls, South Dakota. When I stepped off the airplane, Bishop Dudley was standing there. I had not seen him since the early '70s. I wasn't even sure if I would recognize him. But there he was at the end of the concourse, and he looked at me and immediately knew who I was. This was what I had been desiring all these years away from the Catholic Church. I wanted to be fathered.

Bishop Dudley looked at me, reached out to me with both arms wide, and said, "Welcome home, Jeff." He was like a father who I had walked away from years ago. I returned his warm embrace and we drove back to the bishop's quarters where we — Bishop Dudley, his co-adjutor Bishop Robert Carlson, and I — talked late into the night about my future as a Catholic.

I explained to them my whole testimony in detail and how I'd come to this point. I was totally blind as to what opportunities there might be for me as a Protestant pastor returning to the Catholic Church. After all, when I had left the Catholic Church there was nothing for laypeople to do, and certainly nothing that would support a husband with a wife and family.

I said, "Bishop, I want to come back into the Church but I don't know what to do. I don't know where to go."

He replied, "Jeff, you don't need to worry. There will be a place for you in the Catholic Church." He hinted that there may be possibilities of work in Sioux Falls or someplace else. But whatever happened, he kept reassuring me that there will be a place for me. It felt a little bit like Abraham leaving Ur. It seemed as though the Holy Spirit was saying, "Just get up and leave. Get up and do this. There will be a place for you." I realized it really was a matter of faith. (Not that Bishop Dudley had any intention of not putting his money where his mouth was. In fact, [though he would never dream of saying anything about it himself] the good bishop went on to support our family off and on out of his own personal finances for the next couple of years, sending his checks now and then for a couple of hundred dollars when things became tight. He is a very godly man for whom I am eternally grateful.)

As we talked, I mentioned to him my desire to possibly return to radio — maybe Catholic radio — as a possible way of making a living and combining it with some kind of work for the Church.

But Bishop Dudley said, "Jeff, I think you need to go to Franciscan University. It's a solid university, and you need to be refreshed in your Catholic faith and submitted to the good teaching of the Church before you launch out in that way."

So I had some decisions to make. And above all, I had to decide whether I was really going to return to the Church or not.

That night, in the bishop's quarters, I spent many sleepless hours pacing and thinking. Some people have conversion experiences that are full of sweetness and light. Mine was full of anguish and agony. I felt absolutely alone in the world. I walked round and round the room, looking at all these pictures of saints that hung there. However, as the night wore on I finally came to a point of decision: I would stop thinking about returning to the Catholic Church and *return*. It was clear to me that God had called me home. Now, like it or not, I needed to respond. I must — say yes to my Lord. And so, on a dark cold night in the middle of the winter of 1995, I resolved to come back to the Catholic Church.

The next morning, Bishop Dudley invited me to attend Mass in his chapel.

So I came back from Sioux Falls with a solid decision to return to the Catholic Church. However, Emily was still not thrilled about any of this. Realizing this, I knew also that I needed to be thoughtful and tender with her. So I relented on my more enthusiastic pushiness about the Church, while resolving in my own heart the step that I would take. This seemed to be the wisest thing to do since,

as leader of the family, I needed to take a step based on
the truth rather than on the majority vote of my family,
yet at the same time, I didn't want to force anything on
Emily's conscience.

In addition to this, of course, there still remained the
problem of how I was going to earn my keep when I
came into the Church. Bishop Dudley's counsel to me about
getting an education and grounding in Catholic theology
at Franciscan University at Steubenville seemed somewhat
impractical and I was unsure about whether I really wanted
to do it. So while I investigated the masters of theology
program at Steubenville, I also attempted to cover my bases
by calling Marcus Grodi again and picking his brain some
more. As it happened, Marcus had recently spoken to a
Catholic businessman in Cleveland, Ohio, who was starting a new Catholic radio station. Given my background in
radio, Marcus agreed to put us in contact with each other.
So a few days later this gentleman called me and told me
he was interested in interviewing me for the job of morning talk-show host.

This made me extremely excited. I thought (and pardon the Catholic expression), "Bingo!" I instantly assumed
God was giving me the opportunity to do the broadcasting
I love to do and to alloy it with Catholic theology (and,
in the process, bag the Catholic education at Steubenville
and go straight to Cleveland).

I talked to Emily about that and she said, "Well, check
it out and see what you think." So I flew to Cleveland, met
with the owner, went out to eat, talked about the vision
for the radio station, and things went tremendously well.
He was very excited and so was I. And at the end of the
interview, the owner told me that tomorrow morning, as

a sort of final field test for the interview process, I would simply take over the morning show and do it. So the next morning, there I was: on the air and running the whole morning show. I ran the talk show, answered questions, interviewed people, etc., for several hours. And when I went off the air, the owner met me in his office and said, "The job is yours if you want it."

It all looked so perfect, so providential, so divinely inspired. Bishop Dudley had suggested I go off to Steubenville and get a Catholic education. But that meant going into debt to do it. Now, suddenly, there was this golden opportunity falling into my lap: a talk radio job for the asking in one of the largest Catholic markets in the country. I thought at the moment my choice was obvious.

But that night I went back to my hotel room in Cleveland (overlooking the Rock and Roll Hall of Fame) and began (for the first time really) to pray as well as think about this. There were a lot of things stirred up in me at that moment. In addition to Bishop Dudley's counsel and my worries about our financial state, I was also thinking about Emily and, in particular, Emily's mom.

I stood there thinking to myself, "I need to let my mother-in-law know about this." In all this struggling turmoil, I had not communicated with her much about what I was thinking of doing. So I phoned her and began to tell her about all the struggles with the faith that I had been going through and the decisions that I was trying to make.

She said, "Oh, I understand! I understand!"

Then finally, I screwed up my courage and said, "Alice, I believe I'm coming back into the Catholic Church. In fact, I . . . I *am* coming back."

There was a long pause on her end of the phone.

"So . . ." I said, "what do you think?"

She said, "Well, uh, I . . . I guess that's fine." But the pauses and hesitance in her voice told a different story.

We talked for about an hour on the phone that night and she was unusually quiet. Sometimes, I could hear her sniffling a little bit. She was crying and didn't want me to know. Later, she told me that it was because the realization had hit her very hard: "My daughter is probably going to become Catholic too — and my grandchildren." This shook her badly and that, in turn, shook me. When I got off the phone, I walked over to the window and stood looking out at the downtown area. I stood there thinking about the radio job and about what the bishop had told me. Was I going to go from a conversion based on all my own studies straight into Catholic ministry and on the front lines of apologetics on radio (which would take care of all the bills)? Or was I going to take a year or two to soak myself in the life of the Catholic Church and submit myself to Catholic teaching and further study (which would put us into debt)?

I had seldom felt more acutely the need for God's guidance. So I knelt down right then and there and I prayed. I said, "God, you've gotta lead me. You've *got* to lead me in this. Should I stay in Cleveland and take a talk radio job?"

There in that lonely hotel room, all of a sudden something came over me and I felt absolutely awful! The sense of darkness in my spirit became so thick you could cut it with a knife. It was as though a cloud blocked out the sun and some deep voice within was saying, "NO! NOT CLEVELAND!"

I thought to myself, "Why Lord? Why? I'm coming into the Church. I will soon lose my job as a pastor. Radio is about the only thing I'm trained in. I'm handed a talk radio show in one of the largest Catholic markets in the United States. Why do I not have peace about this? Why?"

At that point, I felt the Lord was saying to me in my heart, "Jeff, if you continue in this vein without submitting yourself to the formal teaching of the Church and to qualified teachers and pastors in the Church, you will be continuing what you have done all along. You will be a teacher unto yourself."

When the Lord said this, something in me came to a decision. I resolved in my heart, "I need to take some time, honor what my bishop has asked me to do, submit myself to the Church, and *learn*." That meant, crazy as it seemed, no income, going into debt, and, as a man in my thirties, uprooting my family to go to Steubenville and start all over.

I knelt there, crying and saying, "God, you've gotta help me!" I had no worldly peace about it, yet at the same time I knew now with certainty the next step I had to take. So I called home and told Emily what had happened. I told her it felt like I was on Mount Moriah and I had just put my beloved son Isaac on the altar — and it was killing me. Yes, I was trained for radio. Yes, this was what I wanted to do since I was a little boy. Yes, I was coming back into the Church. Yes, God had handed me all of this. And yet, I knew in my bones that I was supposed to lay the whole thing on the altar and offer it back to God. So soon thereafter I thanked the owner for his gracious offer but told him that I just couldn't accept it. The only thing that kept me going was the conviction that God had something ahead.

Now up until now, I hadn't let anybody in my church know about any of this. In oblique ways, I'm sure some of them knew something weird was going on. After all,

I couldn't stop reading the *Catechism* and couldn't stop preaching from it. But at the same time, my confusion about where I was going and my fear of what would become of our family and our future if I blabbed too much had kept me rather quiet about these matters. In the back of my mind was the nagging little voice saying, "What if this doesn't work out? Then you'll have spoiled everything! Don't terrify everybody with dramatic announcements of conversions until you have a better sense of where you're going and whether all this stuff is really true." But on the other hand, of course, I felt rather uncomfortable about that. I loved the people I was pastoring. I had a good relationship with them and they with me. By this time, the church split had already taken place and the church I was pastoring were the people who had stuck with me.

Still, they were starting to wonder, "What is happening with him?" Because, of course, I was dying to share with them — particularly with those who had been raised Catholic — everything I had discovered. I wanted to sit down, reason with them, and talk about their faith and the longing of their hearts.

So I had, in previous months, started trying to share with some of the elders the arguments for liturgy, the Catholic understanding of sacred Tradition, and so forth, just to kind of feel them out and see if they were open to it a little bit. That, however, didn't fly very well since it was too dangerously "religious" as opposed to being truly spiritual. Nonetheless, we retained some of the changes I had made to our charismatic service in order to accommodate some liturgy and readings as I mentioned earlier. And above all, we continued to practice communion weekly — which put me in a bind.

I was, after all, the one who had pushed for frequent communion. But my studies of Scripture were leading me to awkward conclusions. In the Old Testament, it was now quite obvious to me that you could not play games with the sacrifice God offers or the worship He requires. Way back in Genesis 22, when Abraham was about to sacrifice Isaac on Mount Moriah, Isaac asked, "Where is the lamb for a burnt offering?" And Abraham, in faith, replied, "God will provide himself the lamb for a burnt offering." Then, just as he is about to sacrifice Isaac as God commanded, God stops him and there in the thicket is a ram — not a lamb — caught by its horns. And, in a curious way, this is the whole Old Testament experience. Throughout the whole Old Testament, Israel is *looking for the lamb*. The people of God are searching for the real Lamb of God who will take away the sins of the world. The Jews, for example, were commanded to take a spotless lamb on the tenth day of Nisan and inspect it until the fourteenth day of Nisan. Then, at twilight, they were to sacrifice that lamb. Under the old covenant, that was that. You could not go to Moses and say, "Hey, we're members of People for the Ethical Treatment of Animals and we don't get into that kind of thing, but we have some cookies shaped like little lambs. So we will just use those and everyone will still get the meaning and the 'spiritual sense' of what you are trying to say here, Moses." You simply could not do that. At the first Passover, that helpful suggestion would have cost you your firstborn when the angel of death passed through Egypt and spared only the house with the blood of the lamb on the lintels and door posts. God was very serious about the necessity of the blood of the lamb.

Yet at the same time, of course, there is the awareness

that though the sacrificial law of Moses must be kept, it cannot take away the sin of the world. In the words of the letter to the Hebrews,

> For since the law was but a shadow of the good things to come instead of the true form of these realities, it can never, by the same sacrifices which are continually offered year after year, make perfect those who draw near. Otherwise, would they not have ceased to be offered? If the worshipers had once been cleansed, they would no longer have any consciousness of sin. But in these sacrifices there is a reminder of sin year after year. For it is impossible that the blood of bulls and goats should take away sins (Hebrews 10:1–4).

So the Passover celebration, in addition to looking back at the first Passover, also looked forward to something greater than itself: something that could do in reality what it could only do symbolically.

In other words, the blood of lambs is not the Blood of the Lamb. It too was a mere shadow or image of the coming reality in Christ. That is why the Old Testament is one long search for the True Lamb and that is why, when John the Baptist appears on the scene, practically the first words out of his mouth after the baptism of Jesus are, "Behold, the Lamb of God, who takes away the sin of the world!" (John 1:29). Jesus is the True Lamb which God Himself has at long last provided.

All the symbolism of the Old Testament points at Jesus in this eerie and yet satisfying way. For example, when the Temple was built in Jerusalem it became more and more difficult (particularly after the Babylonian Captivity and the Diaspora) for pilgrims to Jerusalem during the Passover to bring with them a lamb for sacrifice. There's no way you could get a cute little perfect and spotless lamb all the way from, say, Alexandria to Jerusalem and keep him cute, perfect, and spotless. He'd be pretty ragged. So the Jews instituted what was called the "sacrificial flock." This was a flock of sheep raised in the Jerusalem area and sold to pilgrims at Passover so they would have a lamb to offer. Now the interesting thing is this: that sacrificial flock was brought in through the gates of Jerusalem on the tenth of Nisan for inspection and sale to the pilgrims. The tenth of Nisan corresponds to what Christians refer to as "Palm Sunday." In other words, at the same time the sacrificial flock was entering Jerusalem on the tenth of Nisan, the Lamb of God was coming in, riding on a donkey. Then, Pilate, after inspecting Jesus as the Temple priests examined the lambs, proclaims concerning Jesus, "I find no crime in him" (Luke 23:4). Finally, the Lamb of God is sacrificed at the same hour as the Passover is slaughtered in the Temple. The symbolic connection between the old and new covenants is clear.

But what is not as clear today as it should be is this: the symbolism of the Old Testament does not point us to more symbols. It points us to reality. As Paul says, "These are only a shadow of what is to come; but the substance belongs to Christ" (Colossians 3:17). All the symbolic sacrifices and offerings of the Old Testament were leading us, not toward still more symbols and foreshadowings in the New Testament, but to the reality of God incarnate. And so, on the night before He died, Jesus took bread and wine and gave us, not yet another symbol, but the reality. "This *is* my body. This *is* my blood," he declared. Not a symbol, not a step backward into more shadows and hints, but a step forward into His incarnate sacramental presence in the midst of His Church. And just as, under the old covenant, you couldn't play games with the sacrifice God offers or the worship He requires, so it was under the new covenant. This body God had prepared for Jesus to offer on the cross and raise from the dead was the very same body being offered to all of us through the Eucharist.

And I knew that.

Yet in our church, the bread of communion was still regarded as only a symbol (which indeed it was). Essentially what we said concerning the Old Testament types and shadows of the lamb was, "The reality is coming in Christ! You must look to the New Testament for the fulfillment of this mere symbol." But then, when we looked to the New Testament we were insisting that the fulfillment of the ages had given us . . . another mere symbol and not the reality.

It was a complete anticlimax and reversal of everything Scripture was pointing toward. Worse still, it was a reversal and kind of undoing of what God did in the Incarnation. For as the Letter to the Hebrews tells us, "when Christ came into the world, he said, 'Sacrifices and offerings thou hast not desired, but a *body hast thou prepared for me*'" (Hebrews 10:5). We insisted that we participated in the sacrifice of Christ "spiritually." That is, Communion wasn't really His Body and Blood nor did it need to be. The only thing that mattered was "spiritual" (i.e., disembodied) communion with Jesus. But it was not "spiritual" blood that Jesus shed on the cross. It was real blood. And it was not a disembodied body that came out of the tomb, ate with His disciples, and was touched by Thomas. It was the glorified and altogether real body of Christ. In short, everything in the trajectory of Scripture from the Old Testament to the New pointed to the Eucharist, not as yet another symbol, nor as a disembodied "spiritual" communion, but as our "participation" in the actual Body and Blood of Christ Himself (1 Corinthians 10:16). This was the plain language of the New Testament and, as I had discovered, it was also the plain language of the early Church Fathers, the medieval Church, the Renaissance and early modern Church, and the Catholic Church today. The early Church Fathers were important to me as the Church leaders who preserved the unity of the Faith during the first six centuries. These Church Fathers were heirs to the apostles and gave their lives for the integrity of the Faith. I realized that the Catholic Church, with remarkable consistency, teaches today essentially the same thing said by Ignatius of Antioch in his *Letter to Smyrnaeans*, that "the Eucharist is the flesh of our Saviour Jesus Christ, Who suffered for our sins and which, in His goodness, the Father raised [from the dead]."

I was filled with the growing awareness that, just as you had to eat the Passover lamb in the old covenant, so too must you eat the Passover Lamb of the New.

Yet, there I was, still handing out this symbolic communion with the uncomfortable awareness that I should be receiving the true Eucharist and not handing out facsimiles of it to other people. This bothered me more and more as it became plain to me that I did not have the apostolic power (granted through the sacrament of holy orders and not by virtue of my sincerity) to consecrate a valid communion. For as I well knew from my study of Jewish roots, the New Testament apostolic priesthood, like the Old Testament Levitical priesthood, depended on orderly succession and not on some broad quasi-democratic claim by anyone and everyone to be a priest.

That knowledge increasingly frazzled my nerves and distracted me. As a result, one day, when everybody came up to the altar, I looked down at this lady, an ex-Catholic like so many in our church, gave her a piece of the bread, and, without even thinking about it, used words I didn't normally say.

"The Body of Christ," I said.

She looked up at me, said, "Amen," and made the Sign of the Cross.

I stared at her and said, "What?"

She became flustered and said, "Oh! I'm sorry."

We both blushed. I reassured her that it was okay but thought to myself, "Wow! What's happening here? I shouldn't have said that!" It was "worlds in collision" again.

Finally, I decided I needed to share all of this with a couple of elders from the church, to tell them what was happening in my heart and that I really felt God was calling me back to the Catholic Church. So I called Dave Dahm, one of the elders, and said, "I need to talk to you." Dave was a former Catholic who had, at one time, been a brother in a religious order. I talked to him and his wife, Gundy, and said, "Something is happening in my life and I just have to bounce it off you." Until now, nobody had any clear idea what was going on inside me and I felt I had to be honest with my congregation.

So I said, "I think God is leading me back to the Catholic Church." (Actually, I *knew* He was leading me back but I was worried about shocking them.)

"Really?" they whispered in amazement.

I said, "Yeah!" And I told them exactly what had been happening to me, what God had been doing in my life, and how I'd studied the *Catechism* and bought Scott and Kimberly Hahn's book *Rome Sweet Home*, among many others. I finished by reiterating, "I really feel like God is calling me back to the Catholic Church."

In a hushed voice, Dave told me, "Jeff, the same thing is happening to *us*! I have been privately praying the rosary!" Then Gundy added hesitantly, "God showed me a vision of Mary and gave me a sense of who she is!"

And I had been worried about shocking *them*!

After we finished speaking, I called another elder from my church. He too was a former Catholic. We made an appointment and met and I said, "I need to explain to you what's been happening in my life," and told him the story too.

When I was finished, he said, "Jeff, let me tell you something. Lately, at night, when I can't sleep, I've been praying the rosary."

I thought, "Whoa! What is happening?" Here I was, a pastor of an independent church, and some of my elders were praying the rosary and having visions about Mary! Everywhere I turned, there seemed to be people in my church who were going through the same thing I was going through! There seemed to be this growing hunger for the Catholic Church and for the things of the Catholic Church. Like so many others I have since met, I was out of the Catholic Church, but I couldn't get the Catholic Church out of me. I was flabbergasted!

And it was no longer possible or right to keep it a secret.

One Word

After I finished talking with the two elders, they told me I needed to have a meeting with all the elders. As a result of that meeting, I stepped down from the pulpit and the church sent me on a sabbatical to San Antonio, Texas, in February 1995, saying, "You need to pray about this."

The place were I had my sabbatical was beautiful, a little cabin called the "House of Prayer" located right in the middle of the wilderness. So I sat there all day long for about five days, praying and watching dozens of deer troop past my window. I spent most of that time fasting, praying, and reading again and again, often until one or two in the morning. But the more I prayed, read, and looked at my life, the more certain I was that God was calling me back into the Catholic Church.

When I returned from Texas, I met with the elders and said, "I've really made my decision. I'm leaving the pastorate and I'm going to go back into the Catholic Church." I was reasonably certain of my return to the Church back when I visited Sioux Falls, but one has a tendency to make these types of decisions in steps: by first deciding, then deciding, then deciding again.

They said, "We need to pray for you." They were thinking, "Maybe Jeff's having problems. Maybe he's suffering from the wounds of the church split." They were willing to support me no matter what I did, but they also hoped I would not be deceived, that I would come to my senses about all this. So they called a prayer meeting for me. However, I didn't realize it was a prayer meeting until we arrived there that night. (I thought we were going for coffee and pie.)

So we walked in and there were about forty people lining the walls, all praying — for me! They went around the circle, praying. As they did, I became more tied up in knots inside. Sometimes people will tell you that when you are in the will of God there is just this wonderful sense of peace. Well, I *knew* I was in the will of God but there certainly was no sense of peace. There was just a lot of tension. I have no doubts at all about the genuine love that the people there had for us. If there have ever been people who authentically cared for and loved us it was this group of people. Yet at the same time, though I sensed their love and care, I was also filled with frustration that they could not see what I saw (and that some people were simply closed to the whole idea merely because it was Catholic).

Part of this was due to the odd vacuum-like silence that seemed to surround us whenever I tried to discuss my *reasons* for what I was doing. I kept thinking to myself, "Why is nobody refuting me?" I remembered remarking to a close friend, "Why isn't anybody arguing with me doctrinally about why I shouldn't become Catholic?" It seemed to me that there were two reasons for it. First, I was their pastor and they had real respect and love for me. Nobody enjoys arguing and contradicting someone they love on something so important. But secondly, I genuinely think I was persuasive in my arguments. (My wife Emily suggests a third reason: namely, "When Jeff has his mind made up you're not going to change it!" However, I like to think the first two reasons are better ones. At least I hope so.)

At any rate, at the end of that prayer meeting, two crucial things happened.

First, my best friend, Dwight, came over to me when

everyone was done praying and said, "Jeff, I have to tell you something. Every time I'm around you for the last three or four weeks one word comes to mind."

I looked at him with a start. "What's that?" I asked. "Rebellion."

I said, "What do you mean 'rebellion'?"

He said, "I don't know. It's just that every time I pray for you or think about you, that's the word that comes to mind."

At that point I thought, "Oh. He's hinting at my not being a pastor. That I'm rebelling against my calling as a pastor."

"Gee, thanks," I thought. "That's nice. 'Rebellion'."

Shortly after this, another friend named Kathy came up to me, completely independently of Dwight or the group, and said, "Jeff, the Lord has shared a word with me that I'm supposed to give to you. It is this: the Lord is going to give you a word in the future and when you hear that word, it's going to set you free."

I said to her, "When you say 'a word' do you mean a prophecy of some kind or a single word?"

She said, "One word."

I left that night extremely discouraged because I thought that the people were sort of playing charismatic mind games to put a guilt trip on me. It was ironic really; so much of their resistance to what I now believed about the Catholic Church was due to the fact that they were good students. Much of what they now believed against the Catholic Church, I had once taught myself.

A few weeks went by, and my wife and I were scheduled to lead a teaching tour to Israel on March 7, 1995. I was planning on going on the trip with one of my mentors, Dr. Marvin Wilson, from Gordon College. In an odd way, I was looking forward to the trip with Dr. Wilson because a small part of me was still open to someone punching a hole in my arguments. My doubts were few, but my hunger for truth kept me open to correction. So the plans were set and the day before we were to leave for Israel, my mother flew into Dayton, Ohio, to watch our daughter, Carly.

On that Saturday night, the day before we left, we had everything packed and ready by the door before we went to bed that night. (My mother was sleeping on the hide-a-bed in the living room.) At 3:48 a.m. the telephone rang. Both Emily and I awoke, but we were so fuzz-brained that we just sat looking at each other and mumbling, "Answer that!" to each other. Suddenly, I heard the answering machine in the kitchen pick it up.

A voice came on the line saying, "This is Southdale Fairview Hospital in Edina."

Edina was near where my folks lived.

My dad had had a bypass at age 48. Now he was 59. I had feared for years that my dad was going to have a heart attack. And I thought, "Oh, God!"

My mother came flying into our bedroom and she said, "Jeff! Dad has had a heart attack!"

I went numb. I thought, "Oh, God! What am I going to do?" Despite my anger over my spiritual run-ins with my dad, we loved each other very much. The thought of losing him was almost unbearable. I was frightened for my dad, but I was also thinking, "I'm supposed to leave in just a few hours and there's a bunch of people going to Israel with us! And they are going because they want to go with us. Now what?"

I called the hospital but couldn't get hold of my dad because he was in intensive care. We didn't know how bad it was or anything. Pacing around our apartment exhausted and totally stressed, we kept trying to call until finally we reached dad. Taking the phone, I said, "Dad, how bad is it?"

"They're doing some tests," he said weakly, "they don't know." I was relieved just to hear his voice.

I said, "Mom's heading back in the morning. Should I come, too?"

He said, "Jeff, go ahead and go to the Holy Land." But then after a pause he added, "Jeff, do me a favor."

"Yes?" I queried intently.

"Watch over your mother and your sisters for me."

I made up my mind right then, telling myself, "I can't go to the Holy Land! I've got to be with my dad!"

I said, "Dad, I'm coming home."

"Okay," he said, sounding pleased at my decision.

Emily and I flew out to Minnesota a few hours after my mom. My dad had his second coronary bypass surgery. Dr. Wilson led the trip to Israel without us.

By the third day in Minneapolis, my mind was just swirling. My whole life felt like it was just upside-down. The people of my church were oddly silent toward us, but the Catholic Church had yet to embrace us. I didn't know what to do. In my confusion, I went to St. Edward's Catholic Church in Bloomington, the parish I grew up in until I was fourteen. I went in the middle of the day and just sat there in the back, contemplating my whole life up to that point. I remembered growing up, being confirmed, all the times I'd sat there listening to Fr. Dudley's homilies. I thought about all I was risking in returning to the Catholic Church and all I was risking in not returning. I thought, "I need to talk to someone. Have I made the right decision?" When you are dealing with your whole family and your career, and stepping out into what appears to be nothing, you want to make sure you are right.

I decided to call my friend Wes Wheatley. I had been his pastor at Open Arms in Minneapolis. He was a Lutheran pastor who was a professional counselor. I reached him on the phone and said, "Wes, this is Jeff Cavins."

He beamed into the phone, "Jeff! How are you doing?"

"Oh, fine," I said. (*Liar!*)

After a pause, I went on, "I need to talk to you, Wes. There are some things happening in my life and I just need to run them by someone and get an opinion."

He said, "About what?"

"Wes," I replied, "I think I'm coming back into the Catholic Church."

He said eagerly, "Let's talk tonight," and invited Emily and me over to his house.

That night, we sat down together with Wes and his wife, Gretchen, and he said, "What's going on? Tell me about this Catholic thing."

So I told him from the beginning what had happened in my life and how I was convinced that God was calling me back into the Catholic Church. I explained to him what happened in North Dakota, when I stood up in front of Bishop Driscoll, and clapped my hands together, and said, "I'm done with the Catholic Church! I've had it with the Catholic Church!"

Now I hadn't told Wes anything about that recent prayer meeting with the two people who gave me their words of knowledge. But right in the middle of my explanation, Wes became all excited. He was perched right on the edge of his seat, licking his lips rapidly over and over. And he said, "Jeff! One word! One word!"

I said, "What?"

"One word . . . Rebellion!"

"*What?!*" I gasped as the words of Dwight and Kathy echoed in my mind.

Wes continued in a loud voice, "Jeff, it's as clear as the nose on your face. *Rebellion! You have rebelled against the Catholic Church and against your father.*"

When he said that, it was like scales dropped from my eyes. I was aware that I was on a spiritual journey. I was aware that God was leading me. I was aware that the spiritual jigsaw puzzle was coming together. But this was the first time that I was faced with the idea that much of my ministry had been performed with an underlying spirit of rebellion. The whole thing came rushing back like it was just yesterday, and I just began weeping.

I remember clutching my head and saying, "My God! What have I *done?*" I hadn't left the Church based on a bunch of theological reasons. I had left out of *rebellion.* And for the last fifteen years, I had tried to build the Church myself. I had tried to prove to my dad that I could do it. I had said in my heart of hearts that I didn't need the Catholic Church and I didn't need a priest and I didn't need a father. I was confronted with myself: that I was a rebellious son. I had come into the charismatic movement and been "born again" and no one had understood me. So I had gotten angrier and angrier because of it. And I had left the Catholic Church — and left my father.

I lay there and I just wept and wept and wept. It was as if much of the pain just rolled off me.

Finally, Wes looked at me and said, "You know what you have to do, don't you?"

"I need to repent."

So there I was, face-to-face with my Lutheran minister friend telling me, "You need to repent of leaving the Catholic Church, and you need to repent to your father."

Repentance

The next day my dad was well enough to come home from the hospital. We all came down to the breakfast table. My heart was just pounding. I sat and looked at him. He didn't know what was going on in my life other than that I was starting to look a little bit into the Catholic Church. I had given him some signs that I was open to the Catholic Church. Finally, I worked up my courage and said, "Dad, I need to talk to you about something." My chest tightened and my voice began to crack.

He said, "Yes?"

My mind raced back to that night that I had left home. I literally struggled for a minute or two to get the words out of my mouth as I attempted to articulate my confession. Finally I began, "Dad . . . I . . . Dad . . . I . . . I" The words would not come out.

"What's the matter, Jeff?" Dad asked.

I raised my hand to signal I needed a moment. I began again. "Dad . . . I . . . rebelled against you and I need to repent." It was like pulling the words from my heart with forceps. I went on, my voice trembling, "I want to come back to the Catholic Church."

He looked at me and said, "You don't know what this means to me. I came into the Catholic Church when I married your mother, and we paid a price for it. My parents were Protestants and they didn't understand. There was a lot of conflict between us in the area of religion, and we were never able to settle it to the day they died. But you and I have been able to settle this."

I nodded at him trying hard to contain myself. Each person in the room — Dad, Mom, Emily, and I — was walking through emotional territory where none of us had been before.

Dad went on, "As long as we're getting things off our chests, I need to talk to you about something."

I wondered what he was about to say.

After a pause, he continued, "Do you remember that night you left home?"

I swallowed hard. Suddenly and without warning that seventeen-year-old scab was being ripped open. "Yes," I said.

He said, "I'm so sorry. I'd never hit you before." His voice became very soft and hesitant. "I . . . I don't know what got into me. I couldn't talk any sense into you, so I thought maybe I could knock some sense into you. I'm so sorry, so sorry." He went on, "But what has really hurt me all these years is what you said to me after that."

I could not for the life of me remember what I had said that night. I asked with concern, wondering what I could have said to him that hurt him all these years, "What was it? What did I say?"

His voice shaking with emotion, Dad said, "When you were laying on the floor after I knocked you down, you looked up at me and pointed at my face. Then you yelled, 'You're no father of mine!'" I could see that his physical body hurt as much from these words as from his surgery. "It's hurt all these years," he cried.

It all came back to me like it was yesterday. I could not believe that I had buried that awful declaration for so long! "Oh Dad," I choked, stumbling around the table to hug

him. "I'm sorry! I *am* your son and you *are* my father."
The four of us cried together, exchanging hugs of recon-
ciliation, each of us touched by the freedom and healing
of forgiveness.

A tremendous healing took place in my life after that.
From that point the pull of God back into the Catholic
Church was stronger than ever. After that day, for months,
there was hardly a week that would go by when my parents
wouldn't call me and talk about Jesus. They went through
a Cursillo (a weekend retreat that focuses on growing in
our relationship with Christ). Then they *really* wouldn't
stop talking about Jesus. My mother told me, "Not one
Mass went by these years when I didn't pray for you to
come back to the Catholic Church." Mom was, quite simply, ecstatic and giddy about my return. As for my dad, one
typical example of how he has changed is that just before
Christmas 1995 he called and said, "Jeff, this Christmas
let's not focus on gifts, let's focus on Jesus." This was my
father! Since then, we have talked about the Lord a great
deal.

For Emily's part, through all this, she was saying she
understood why I wanted to come back into the Catholic
Church. She said she disagreed with some of the doctrine
but that she would work with it and try to understand. I
didn't want her to convert just because I was returning.
In fact, I told her, "Honey, don't convert to the Catholic
Church unless, if I die right after that, you will remain
Catholic because of your own convictions. I want this to
truly be your decision. I want you to own it, not just go
along with me."

Emily, bless her heart, committed to doing just this,
which was a real act of sacrificial love after a strenuous
life of changes in church affiliation. In her childhood, her

family had moved through various denominations. Then after I had declared to the bishop in North Dakota that I was no longer Catholic, she had barely given Catholicism or traditional churches a second thought. However, after the twelve years of independent churches we pastored, she also had begun to see the problems of trying to lead people when truth and authority are not established. As a teen, she had witnessed the fallout from the illicit affair of a pastor in the independent church she attended. She had seen splits in many Baptist churches. Most recently, she had endured firsthand the painful split at NCF. So she also had been excited about the liturgy and life of the Charismatic Episcopal Church. She had thought we were on the same page until the day I casually mentioned, "You know, I've been looking into the Catholic Church." That, it seemed to her, was just one jolt too many. She saw that her world was about to change forever, and there was little she could do about it. She imagined losing all our friends and life just becoming foreign. It was okay to go as far as the Episcopal church because that was still Protestant, but *Catholic*! So it was a real act of courage for her to take that step of faith and consider the possibility nonetheless.

She knew I had to do what I was convinced of, so she bore it graciously as I journeyed back to the Church. She was happy for me personally, but she dreaded what it meant for our family. She, like me, didn't want us to be divided in faith. She was not opposed to leaving Dayton in order to move to Steubenville, Ohio. In fact, she was glad to move and get away from the uncomfortable situation we had been in for too many months. She was ready for a fresh start. So, after some time, she agreed to attend the Rite of Christian Initiation for Adults (RCIA) program at Franciscan University, and after that, if she could honestly say,

"I want to be Catholic," then she would join the Church. That made me happy. Very happy.

Soon after, on April 19, 1995 (I remember it because it was the day of the Oklahoma City bombing) I called Franciscan University at Steubenville and told them I was coming.

Then I told the elders I needed to put in my resignation formally. So I gathered the church together and explained this whole story. In tears, I told them that I could not *not* come back into the Catholic Church. And to this, God bless them, they responded with genuine Christian love and kindness, though they did not, of course, agree with me.

Many Confirmations

My last stint as a pastor was to do a wedding on April 22, 1995, in Denver. I didn't want to do it but I had to. I'd given my word. So I flew out to Denver and did the wedding. I was to return on April 23 back to Dayton. I asked the groom, who had given me what's called a "buddy pass" (which means you can fly anywhere), "Do you mind if I fly from Denver to Minneapolis to visit with Bishop Dudley and my parents?" (Because by this time we were talking about the Lord every week and I was enormously enjoying time with my parents.)

The groom agreed.

I went to the Continental Airlines desk on the morning of April 23 and said, "I want to go to Minneapolis."

They said, "We don't have a direct flight to Minneapolis."

I said, "Oh. Well then, how else can I get there?"

They said, "You have to fly to Newark, New Jersey, or Houston, Texas, and *then* back to Minneapolis."

Hmmph.

I said, "Then I'll try Houston."

They looked at the screen. "It's all booked up already. You are going to have to fly out to Newark, New Jersey."

So I flew to Newark and arrived at 1:00 in the afternoon. My flight was at 3:10 p.m. to Minneapolis.

I'm sitting there in the concourse with my hand on my rosary — a Protestant minister with his hand on his rosary.

And I'm praying. At this point in the conversion process I was in a very lonely place. My Protestant friends had fallen into the vacuum-like silence toward me. But I was not reconciled to the Church either and had practically no Catholic friends (except for people who lived far from us). I still had to go through the sacrament of penance. I was just in a sort of limbo. So I'm thinking, "Oh Lord! I could sure use some fellowship. I just feel so lonely."

At length, I decided to go check and see if my flight was on time. So I went to the screen and looked for the 3:10 p.m. flight. It said, "Canceled." I thought, "Oh no!" I went to the service counter and said, "My flight's canceled! What am I supposed to do?"

They said, "The next flight is at 7:10 tonight."

A six-hour wait. So I went back on the bench, sat down, had my hand on my rosary, and said out loud, "Lord, I could sure use some confirmation in all of this."

Just then, this lady walked by wearing a huge gold crucifix.

"She's got to be Catholic!" I thought to myself. "She's got to be radical! Maybe someone who would talk about the Faith."

I decided I would get up, start following her, see where she sits down, and then strike up a conversation. So I grabbed my bag and started following her around the airport. But she wouldn't sit down. So I just kept wandering around behind her. Finally, however, she just went right out the door of the airport.

I thought, "Awww rats!" Then I turned around — and there to my surprise was a priest sitting on this little bench!

Summoning my mastery of the obvious to its height, I said to myself, "*He's* gotta be Catholic. I'll strike up a conversation with *him*."

I walked over to him nonchalantly and saw that he was praying the rosary. I stood there for a moment and finally said, "Hello, Father!"

"Oh, hi!" he said, and then invited me to have a seat.

I sat down next to him and said, "So . . . where are you traveling to?"

He said, "I'm going to Rome to see the Holy Father."

This was a good start.

"Then," he said, "I'm going to Israel."

I told him I had been to Israel many times and had done some work over there. From here, the conversation proceeded splendidly, though we had not yet exchanged names.

He said, "What about you? Where are you traveling to?"

"Well," I said, "I'm going from Denver to Minneapolis via Newark." I chuckled, "But my whole life is sort of like that right now. I've been a Protestant pastor for twelve years and I am coming back into the Catholic Church. I'm going to head to Steubenville this summer to take some courses. That's sort of where I'm at right now."

All of a sudden he became excited and scooted forward on the bench. "*I know who you are!*" he exclaimed.

I blinked and felt a crop of Godbumps rising on my skin. (For you who don't know, that's goose bumps for Christians.) I said, "What?!"

He repeated excitedly, "I know who you are! I was just down in Dallas, Texas, and Bishop Paul Dudley told me about you! I'm Bishop Andrew McDonald. I'm the bishop of Arkansas!" He raised his hand and said, "This is confirmation!"

My head was spinning. I said in amazement, "Yeah!"

He said, "I can't believe it! He just told me about you and now . . . here you are! He just told me and . . ." his voice trailed off for a moment. Then he raised his hands and said, "Praise the Lord! Isn't this wonderful?"

I was speechless. We both were for a moment. Those words, "This is confirmation," rang in my head. Then he saw my rosary, grabbed hold of it, and started to bless it. He looked at me and said, "Do you know what I'm doing here?"

I said, "No."

He reached down, pulled out two envelopes from underneath his leg, and said, "I'm supposed to be at Gate 99, but I wanted to mail these two envelopes and put them in that mailbox over there. So I thought, 'I'll just sit on them for five minutes and pray the rosary and then I'll go.' I just wanted to make sure they're good and sealed. So I sat down to pray the rosary . . . and you came over."

"Isn't that something?" he repeated.

I thought, "Wow! God flies you from Denver to Newark, cancels your flight, you follow a cross, and you meet a bishop who knows you and says, 'This is confirmation'!"

I just sat there stunned. A little while ago, I had been sitting there praying, "Lord, I could sure use some confirmation." By now I had reached the point where I was saying, "Okay Lord, I've got it! I don't need any more confirmation."

We wound up talking for two hours, and at the end, the bishop took out a card and wrote to Bishop Dudley:

Paul, here I am in Newark 4–23–95, 3:10 p.m.

3:10 p.m. was when my canceled flight was supposed to have left. He didn't know that. Since that time, I've shown the card to so many people I had to have it laminated because it was getting wrecked.

After that, I was on cloud nine. I said, "God, you really

do love me! You have brought me through this whole battle and brought me back to the Catholic Church!"

At last, on May 30, 1995, Bishop Paul Dudley came to my parents' home in Minneapolis to formally receive me back into the Catholic Church. He had told me to wait all these months and I had. But when at last he came, he brought me to the back porch, and I made a general confession with special emphasis on rebellion, and he granted me absolution and brought me back into the Catholic Church. Bishop Driscoll's first prophecy to me, way back on the morning after I left the Church, was fulfilled.

Then we all went into the dining room — the bishop, my parents, my sister Jayne, Emily, Carly, and me, as well as my Aunt Connie and her son Joe — and there Bishop Dudley celebrated Mass on my parents' table. I was with my family: my parents and the family of God. And when the moment came in the liturgy to extend the peace of Christ to one another, you better believe that was no rote gesture. My parents and I embraced and it was an emotional moment for us all.

In late spring 1995, I went to Steubenville to check out housing for school and I came and stayed at Scott and Kimberly Hahn's house. They hardly knew me, but they said, "Come stay in our house." (That's love, to open up your house to strangers!) And once I was there, Scott and I stayed up all night in the kitchen and worked through doctrinal questions and so forth. In particular, we went through a "Bible timeline" I had created in order to help facilitate Scripture study. The timeline was designed to give readers the picture of the basic books describing the sweep of biblical history from Genesis to Revelation and then to show where various books in Scripture fit into that historical outline. I had originally created the timeline as a result of my Jewish roots studies and had begun teaching it at Open Arms. I had modified and polished it during my days with Dwight Pryor as a tool for helping people grasp the sweep of salvation history. I showed Scott my method of reading the Bible in chronological order by identifying the historical books and reading them in tandem with the non-historical books in their proper place. Scott was really excited by this because his specialty is salvation history. He, in turn, started giving me his ideas on salvation history and we worked together to see how our work could be integrated to make it more clear for his students. So we were like two kids in a candy shop that night and had a terrific visit.

Shortly thereafter, in June, Emily, Carly, and I moved to Steubenville, a small industrial town on the west bank of the Ohio River with a large population of Italian Catholics. We rented a home belonging to Fr. John Bertolucci a few miles from campus. We all experienced feelings of loneliness in different ways: Carly had to face being the new kid at school, Emily was suddenly thrust into an unfamiliar world of Catholicism and I felt the responsibility of making ends meet while attending school.

A few days after moving, I wandered the college campus in contemplation of all that was happening. I sat on a large rock in the middle of the campus and again wondered, "God, have I done the right thing?" I had gone from a place where I was the pastor of a congregation to a place where I knew no one but the Hahns, was going deeply into debt, had uprooted my family, and had no clue where I was going to end up when school was all over. A feeling of great loneliness and doubt settled over me.

Over the summer I had the opportunity to attend the many conferences held on the university campus. The "Defending the Faith" conference was particularly helpful for me. Listening to speakers like Thomas Howard (who I finally was able to meet face-to-face), Karl Keating, and Peter Kreeft really bolstered and confirmed my faith. After the battles I had been through, it was good to find strength, not only in the information provided at the conferences, but in the fact that I was not alone. I began to discover and take great comfort in the fact that there were people both entering and returning to the Church all over the country. It became more and more apparent to me that my journey was not some weird isolated event, but that it was part of a larger movement of the Holy Spirit: God was bringing a lot of people back Home.

Our family was blessed by becoming friends with another professor at the university and his family, Dr. Alan Schreck. He had a daughter Carly's age and they soon became close friends, and his wife Nancy agreed to be Emily's sponsor in the RCIA program which would begin in the fall.

Some other wonderful opportunities opened up for us and soon we did not feel isolated and lonely. Scott Hahn asked me to be his teaching assistant and to fill in for him during his classes when he was out of town. The Hahns were also in need of a secretary at their home office. Emily's skills were just what they needed, so she began working for them as Carly headed off to school. Just before my fall school term began, Kimberly Hahn caught up to me after Mass and said, "Fr. Giles wants to talk to you." Fr. Giles Dimock, OP, was another faculty member at Franciscan University and, it turned out, Scott had told him about the Bible timeline I had created. So I got in touch with Fr. Giles and he asked me, "Would you be interested in teaching your 'Introduction to Scripture' class? We're interested in you teaching your Bible timeline."

I said yes in a heartbeat.

So at the beginning of fall term, I was standing in front of a classroom full of young Catholics, teaching them about Scripture. As a way of opening the class, I shared my testimony with them on the first day. When I came to the part about Bishop Driscoll, it suddenly dawned on me that what he had said to me so long ago — that I would return and teach my people — had come true too. I stopped, gathered myself emotionally, and said to my students in wonder, "That has come to pass today." It was the same weird feeling as at the airport.

Even more amazing, in the fall of 1995, Bishop Dudley contacted Franciscan University to establish a new fund, a scholarship, for Protestant pastors who are returning to the Catholic Church. It's called the "Blessed John Newman Scholarship." And the rebellious kid Bishop Driscoll had once called "Little Newman" was the first recipient. Score three for Bishop Driscoll.

My time at Franciscan University turned out to be an absolutely vital lifeline for me. I credit Franciscan University at Steubenville and its people as an anchor God used to keep me steady during some wobbly early days. For during that time, I had several incidents take place that might have deflected me from the Church or propelled me back out once I was in. Two in particular spring to mind, not only because they were shocking and upsetting to me, but because I have since found that so many people returning to the Church or discovering it for the first time have had similar experiences and not known what to do.

The first took place when I visited a parish in Minnesota just as I was on the verge of conversion. As I walked in the front door of the church, I started noticing that this parish was different from the other parishes I had gone to and was sharply at odds with the teaching of the Church in both the *Catechism* and Scripture. For instance, I found a brochure in the vestibule that talked about the "He/She God" and which seemed to be obsessively focused on what you might call "the pronoun formerly known as 'He'." The pamphlet seemed to have a phobic reaction to calling God "Father" and to any use of a masculine pronoun in speaking of God. It was very weird.

Eventually, I found someone from the parish staff and asked if Fr. So-and-so was there. They went to find him and he came wandering into the sanctuary with no collar or any other clerical garb on. I was taken aback by this and asked if he was the priest. He said yes and we had our meeting, but I came away from the place confused by the obvious and not-so-obvious departures from the Catholic Church I had been studying in books and the *Catechism*.

The confusion was not helped by a second incident that took place as I was sitting on an airplane not long after. I was, at this stage, extremely hungry for any fellowship I could find. So imagine my surprise and delight when, as the plane was loading, a priest approached! I thought to myself, "Great! A priest I can talk with about the Catholic Faith!" And things looked even better when he sat down right next to me! I thought to myself, "Yes!" So I wasted no time and immediately engaged him in conversation.

I told him excitedly that I had come back to the Catholic Church.

He said, "Really!" and then unexpectedly added, "What Church?"

I was baffled by this and replied, "Well, Father, you're Catholic! I mean the Catholic Church of course!"

He answered, "I have to warn you that the current 'Pope' is not really a Pope. In fact, there is no Pope and hasn't been since 1958."

I was dumbfounded. I didn't know what to say to him. I felt like someone had punched me in the stomach.

He went on and on from there, darkly warning me that "the Church is not what you think it is" and claiming secret knowledge about all sorts of sinister conspiracies surrounding the papacy since the time of Pius XII. Then he took out from his briefcase a breviary and a bunch of literature all about the Latin Mass and the evils wrought by the Second Vatican Council (and by Pope John Paul II). Then he went into this whole teaching about the Tridentine rite Mass being the only true Mass and how the Mass promulgated by Pope Paul VI was invalid and so forth.

I sat there listening to him and wondering to myself, "Where is he *coming* from?" At that point, I didn't know how to argue with him. Nor did I feel much inclined to argue with a priest. So I sat there getting more and more confused and discouraged. Here was a *priest* telling me the Pope wasn't really the Pope. Mind you, I was not confused enough to just back out of it, but still I was baffled at the spectacle of a priest rejecting the authority of the Pope. I'd never heard of such a thing.

Finally, I started to explain to him my reasons for coming back into the Catholic Church and that one of the reasons for my decision *was* the Pope. I told him I was looking for that leadership and for the voice of Christ in His vicar. I told him that the ministry, work, and teachings of Pope John Paul II had given me great joy, direction, and comfort. At that point, he started to back off a little bit. But by this time, the damage was done. I stepped off the plane feeling very deflated.

However, not long after, I talked with Scott and several other people at Franciscan University and they explained to me both the problems with the "He/She God" Minnesota parish I visited and the holes in the position of my priest friend on the airplane (a position technically known as "sedevacantism"). The answers essentially consisted of the fact that there is absolutely nothing invalid about the elections of any of the Popes since 1958, nor with the Second Vatican Council, nor with the promulgation of the *novus ordo* Mass. The real problems plaguing the Church are not "false Popes" or an invalid council but are rather bad implementation of the Church's teachings (as, for instance, at the Minnesota parish I visited with its "dissenting" encouragement of the trendy "He/She God") and an hysterical over-reaction to this by a small minority at the opposite end of the spectrum. In other words, I had discovered that the Church, like all human things, had a sensible center (where the Pope lives) and an extreme left and right fringe. The "He/She God" fringe people wa-a-a-ay out on the left were occupying their time obsessing over masculine pronouns, lobbying for sexual license, and griping about the Pope being too conservative. The sedevacantist fringe people waaaay out on the right were occupying their time obsessing over picky details in canon law that "proved" there was no Pope in Rome, lobbying for the overthrow of the Second Vatican Council, and griping about the Pope being too liberal. The thing they had in common was the fact that, just like the Protestantism I had abandoned, both sides were griping about the Pope. Why, it was almost as though both the extreme left fringe and extreme right fringe were just two more species of Protestantism!

Discovering this phenomenon at work in the Catholic Church helped enormously. Essentially it boiled down to the realization that the good news is the Catholic Church was like a big family and that the bad news was the Catholic Church was like a big family. To extremists, what is normal and healthy (for example, Pope John Paul II) is always regarded with suspicion and fear. But when different extremists attack the Pope for diametrically opposite reasons (as the Pope is habitually attacked for simultaneously being too conservative and too liberal), it drove home the point that the Pope, not his attackers, was who I should listen to. As G. K. Chesterton said long ago, "If you hear a thing being accused of being too tall and too short, too red and too green, too bad in one way and too bad also in the opposite way, then you may be sure that it is very good."[1]

But the "family" at Franciscan University was not at the fringe, attacking the Pope. They were very consciously devoted to remaining at the center, standing with the Pope. And because of that, they were a deep and rich source of life, joy, and common sense that helped me get and keep my balance in the midst of these polarizing and destructive influences. For they taught me, above all, to stay with the Holy Father, the descendant of Peter the Rock, to whom Jesus still says, "On this rock I will build my Church and the gates of hell shall not prevail against it" (Matthew 16:18).

This family was also of great help to Emily and ten-year-old Carly, who entered and loved the RCIA program at Franciscan University under the guidance of Professor Barbara Morgan. They provided instructions for Carly at her age level. Emily's questions about the Faith were answered and she learned of its richness. Her hardest hurdle was the concept of Mary as our mother. It was so for-

---

[1] G. K. Chesterton, *Brave New Family* (San Francisco: Ignatius, 1990), p. 122.

eign to her. She understood what the teachings were in her head, but couldn't embrace them completely with her heart. As the time grew nearer to Easter when they were to be brought into the Church, she read more about it and struggled. Finally, as Scott and I recommended, she accepted the Church's teachings on Mary by faith without having to have it all figured out. The Church, she reasoned, had existed far longer than she, so how could she comprehend it all in one year's time?

After Emily and Carly were received into the Church in April 1996, our family felt reunited. Since becoming Catholic some of the things Emily appreciates most about the Church are the liturgy and its yearly cycle, the understanding of the saints as our brothers and sisters who have gone before us and who intercede for us, and the unity of the global Church community under the authority of the Pope. We are grateful that our children now have a heritage.

As far as our relationship with Emily's family, they have been very accepting and have learned more about the Catholic Faith. Emily's mother, who is now a Methodist pastor of two small churches in northern Minnesota, is excited about what we are doing and supports us completely.

As a consequence of the joyful, creative orthodoxy at Franciscan University, there was a spirit of adventure about the faith for which I will always thank God. The theology department was fascinated with Scripture. We had constant discussions about it. More than this, the most important thing I learned at Steubenville was prayer. I learned to go to the Blessed Sacrament regularly and for more than a year Scott Hahn and I had a holy hour nearly every morning. We met and prayed together, we wrestled with issues together, and then we went to the chapel together.

Those were extremely special times for me. Not least because Scott has (as anyone who knows him will tell you) a way about him of discussing Scripture that makes you want to run home, open your Bible, and read it yourself. His enthusiasm for Bible study is enormously contagious, precisely because it is genuine enthusiasm. He is on fire about Scripture and that fire, when you are touched by it, sets you on fire as well.

Scott and I discussed many things during that time. In particular, he stressed to me the importance of frequent confession. Because of this, it was in Steubenville that I learned not only theology and various academic subjects, but the extremely important habits of regular confession and regular prayer. Likewise, it was at Steubenville that I learned the immense value of daily Mass. To put it simply, daily Mass became my life's blood. I could not wait to come before the Lord every single day. And in coming before Him, I found limitless help to do the work of learning and teaching that the Lord was calling me to do — help that came from various and often unexpected directions, such as a little nun with a great big television network. In His quirky way, God made her my last and greatest confirmation.

Stepping into the Future

In May 1996, during my last quarter at Steubenville, I was very busy teaching and taking classes. I was also busy wondering what I was going to do once I graduated. That was worrisome, but those worries and fears were calmed by Fr. Michael Scanlan, TOR, president of Franciscan University, who was and is a great mentor for me. You may recall that way back when I was eighteen years old I had been briefly involved in a Catholic charismatic prayer group before I left the Church. Fr. Scanlan was one of the speakers on the tapes I had listened to and he had always stood out as an example to me of what a disciple of Jesus should look like. When I finally made it to Steubenville, I was thrilled to have a chance to sit down and talk with this man who had meant so much to me and who had left an impression on me even during my long years as a Protestant. During our first meeting, he had said to me something that kept coming back every time I started to fret about the future: "Jeff, the Lord is calling you here. So everything will work out. Don't you worry about it." (Little did I know that part of the reason he was so confident of this was because he was involved with Bishop Dudley in establishing the "Blessed John Newman Scholarship." Fr. Scanlan is not a man to merely talk about love, he lives it.)

So with Fr. Scanlan's words in mind, I kept praying for God to show me the next step to take after graduating. And sure enough, his words were dead on. For in that last quarter I received a phone call from a producer at EWTN, the network that had so providentially elbowed *Your Port-folio* out of my VCR a year or two before. Bishop Dudley had been on the network recently and had suggested they contact me about guesting on one of their shows. The call was a complete surprise.

Mother Angelica, the founder of EWTN, wanted to know if I would be willing to be a guest on her show and tell my story of returning to the Church. At first, I was going to say "no" for the simple reason that I was just swamped with work. We were coming into finals, I was teaching my own class, had family to take care of, and it was all just way too much. But then, as I thought about it, I realized this would be a wonderful opportunity to talk about what God had done in my life. So I prayed about it and decided to tell EWTN "yes."

So on February 28, 1996, I flew to Birmingham, Alabama, was met at the airport by one of the EWTN people, and was taken to stay at Madonna house, one of the guest houses at EWTN. I had no idea what to expect. I didn't know what the show was going to be like. I wondered what Mother Angelica was going to ask me. I spent the evening nervously rehearsing my testimony in my mind as a way of keeping off the jitters. Eventually, the producer came over and did a short interview with me to prepare for the show, then we walked over to the studios.

We entered a large building and I found myself in the green room of the EWTN studio. This is a sort of combination kitchen and waiting room that is located about twenty feet to the left of Mother Angelica when you're watching her on television. A door separates it from the main studio and, as it happened that night, the green room was in quite a bit of chaos due to a remodeling project. I sat down and the makeup guy came over and proceeded to start powdering my mug. That was an odd feeling, but what was even odder was the fact that suddenly cameras were flashing around me everywhere. I looked around and asked someone what was going on. They replied that *Time* magazine was there doing a special story on Mother Angelica and EWTN! I thought to myself, "What have I walked into?"

However, before there was time to figure out an answer, it was ten minutes to air time, and Mother Angelica was now entering the room, supported as ever by her crutches and surrounded by various assistants. We were introduced and she grabbed my hand, gave me a sweet smile, and was the very soul of kindness to me. I was struck by how smooth and soft her skin was. Her eyes were reassuring and grandmotherly.

After exchanging greetings, I said, "So, uh, Mother, what kind of questions are we going to talk about?"

She just smiled and said, "It'll be all right, sweetheart."

I thought (with a slight grin), "Oh great, Jesus. I know how things go when *You* lead! This is gonna be a wild evening!"

But before I had time to fret much, we had all joined hands to pray for the broadcast and then we bustled through the door and into the main studio. The floor director did the countdown, the cameras sprang to life, and to our delight Mother and I discovered that we absolutely clicked. I told my story, she was laughing, she was crying, the whole thing went off as smoothly and beautifully as if it had been scripted. Looking back, I think about how odd it was because she had never met me before, yet, right in the middle of the show and to my complete astonishment, she grabbed my arm and said, "Sweetheart, would you pray about doing a thirteen-week show for us?"

At this, I paused, surprised, yet retained the presence of mind to bend my head down for about one nanosecond, close my eyes, open them again, and say, "Yes!"[1]

Then, as the show ended, Mother did something even more unusual: she took me aside with Michael Warsaw, the senior vice president of EWTN, and said, "Would you pray about moving here and starting your own live show for young adults?"

I thought, "Wow!" It felt like a dream.

I said, "Mother, I'm trained in broadcasting. It's been my life's joy! I've dreamed of doing television!"

She said, "I've been praying about this for fifteen years and the Lord told me you're the one."

I felt sort of dazed and said, "Mother, I'm gonna have to pray about this."

So I returned to Steubenville, and Emily and I spent the next two months praying about it. I met with Bishop Dudley, talked to various spiritual leaders, and as time progressed, it became more and more evident to me that the Lord really was leading me to do the show for young adults at EWTN. So on the last day of classes at Franciscan University (in August 1996), we were on our way to Birmingham.

The reason we left in such a hurry was because EWTN

---

[1] In a funny way, the show Mother asked me to do would just sort of put itself together. My immediate idea was that I would like to do a show on Scripture, followed almost instantly by the thought, "Nobody has ever heard of me, so why would anyone watch it?" However, I soon found out that Scott Hahn was also planning to do a show for EWTN. So I mentioned my idea to him and we quickly found that our ideas married very well. Therefore, we went into creative partnership together and ended up making *Our Father's Plan*, which was, thanks be to God, very well received.

had called to say they were celebrating their fifteenth anniversary on the air and they wanted me to host that show. I kept thinking, "Why me? Why do all these wonderful things keep happening to me? Ever since this journey began, it's been just one thing after another where I'm not *opening* any doors; they just *fly* open and I walk through!" And now, here was Mother Angelica asking, "Will you host my fifteenth anniversary show?" So suddenly, I find myself in the host's chair interviewing people like Fr. George Rutler, Monsignor Eugene V. Clark, Fr. Mitch Pacwa, and on and on. It made my head spin. I was enormously grateful. What an opportunity!

And the opportunities did not stop. EWTN gave me complete free rein to construct the show for young adults however I pleased. I ran an informal poll among some friends at Franciscan University asking for name ideas and somebody came up with *Life on the Rock*. The folks at Franciscan University were thrilled (as was I) at the thought that one of their alumni would host a live Catholic television show, and still more that the show would be aimed at bringing the Faith to young adults.

As time passed, we developed a basic concept of the show, the sets, and general, relaxed "coffeehouse" feel. My producer and I asked several Catholic musicians to write a theme song, as I knew this would be an important component of the show. Joe and Jeanne Ann Hand hit a home run with the tune they submitted. I knew their song "Life on the Rock" was it the moment I heard it. Finally, on January 9, 1997, *Life on the Rock* premiered with my first guest, Mary Beth Bonacci, and the show received both good reviews and good ratings, thanks be to God.

After about six months at EWTN, Scott and I began to develop a weekly radio talk-show with the intention of

broadcasting it over WEWN, the short wave radio network run by EWTN. We had come so far in the develop-
ment of the show, in fact, that we had actually installed all
the broadcast equipment in Scott's house. Mother Angelica
had approved it and signed off on it, so we were excited
and ready to go.

But then I received a sudden and mysterious message
from Mother Angelica that she did not want me to do
the radio show! I was shocked. I thought, "What did I do
wrong?" Had I said or done something on the air? It was
puzzling. So I went to Michael Warsaw and asked what
was going on. He said, "I'm not sure. Mother just said that
she had something for you that you don't know about."
That baffled me.

So another few weeks went by and finally I had a chance
to talk with Mother in her office. At that meeting, she told
me that the reason she didn't want me tied up on Tues-
day nights was that she wanted me to be her substitute on
Mother Angelica Live when she was sick or out of town.

Once again, I was floored. I thought, "Whoa! Everything
just keeps opening up more and more!" I was so honored
and thrilled that I had trouble spluttering out my excited
"Yes! I'd love to!" So a kid who had walked away from the
Catholic Church and rebelled against his father, was now
not only graciously given back his Church and his family,
not only given the privilege of working with Scott Hahn
to proclaim the Gospel, he was now being handed a TV
show on a silver platter, and becoming a substitute host for
Mother Angelica. My mind leapt back to two more weird
incidents in the recent past. The first was that strange moment during my first phone conversation with Scott where,
like a bolt from the blue, he had oddly remarked, "Jeff, I
just have this funny feeling that you and I are going to be

working closely together for a long time." The second was the even stranger moment when, standing in front of the video of the EWTN broadcast that should have been *Your Portfolio*, I had distinctly sensed the Holy Spirit say to me, "This is your future." I had thought at the time that God simply meant He was directing me toward the Catholic Church. Now I realized that God was having Himself a really good chuckle. He really is "able to do far more abundantly than all that we ask or think" (Ephesians 3:20)! The confirmations that had begun in that airport in Newark were now piling up to an almost silly level! It made me feel giddy.

Another giddy (and oddly foreshadowed) moment was when I was asked by EWTN to go to France to cover World Youth Day in August 1997. When Pope John Paul II came into the World Youth Day grounds in his "Popemobile," he passed within ten feet of me. And I stood there with tears just rolling down my cheeks thinking, "This is the man I saw in the video from Mile High Stadium that so touched my heart!" And now here I was, pulled by the grace of God from wrestling on my living room couch with the question of the Catholic Church, all the way across the world to the Eiffel Tower, ten feet away from the Pope and yelling out, "Yea! Go Papa!" I was now doing what that exuberant young girl in the video had done. The Holy Father *was* cool. And it was great! It touched me to my very core that this was the Vicar of Christ.

But, as if this were not enough, one last extraordinary sign of God's loving power in and through His Catholic Church is yet to be told. It happened this way.

For more than forty years Mother Angelica was in constant physical pain because of a chronic spinal condition. As a young novice, she was injured in an accident that left her partially paralyzed for a short time and unable to walk or even stand without crutches for the rest of her life. Although many of her viewers never realized the extent of her suffering because of the humor and joy she radiates on television programs, she was encumbered by a back brace, leg braces, and chronic asthma. Anybody who worked at EWTN was well familiar with the sound of her crutches as she made her way through the hallways of the facility. Mother herself took her continual pain in stride. She viewed it as her participation in the cross of Christ and offered it back to God for His glory. But all of us who know her know how much that had cost her and how much she suffered.

One Wednesday night in February 1998, I was preparing to meet with a man named Mike Manhart, who was scheduled to be my guest on *Life on the Rock* the next night. Unbeknownst to me, Mike had come in early so he could watch Mother Angelica do her show on Wednesday night. (Mother's guest that night was Fr. John Corapi.) However, because I did not know this, when I went to find Mike at the guest house and then on the EWTN grounds, I couldn't track him down. Eventually, I made my way to Madonna house, the main guest house, after Mother's show was over and ran into Fr. Corapi.

As soon as I was in the door, Fr. Corapi looked at me with wide, excited eyes and said, "Did you hear!?"

"Hear what?" I said.

He said, "Mother's *healed*!"

I said, "*What*?"

He said, "Just twenty-five minutes ago! She was healed in her office!"

I studied his face to see if he was kidding and said, "Are you serious?"

He said, "Yes!" Then he proceeded to tell me about a lady who had come from Italy to pray for Mother. He said they were praying the rosary in her office when suddenly the Holy Spirit just filled the room and Mother was completely healed! She had taken off her braces and was *dancing* around the kitchen/green room next to the studio.

That was where Mike Manhart came into the story. It turned out he was busy taking a tour of EWTN after the show. I hadn't found him but the Holy Spirit knew right where he was and deftly steered him into the green room just as Mother Angelica came whirling and twirling out of her office as gleeful as a school girl! She didn't know him from Adam, but that did not give her a moment's hesitation. She grabbed him, danced several turns around the kitchen, and then mischievously asked, "Who are you?"

He said, "I'm Jeff's guest for tomorrow night."

She said, "Oh!" with a laugh and kept dancing for a few more turns. Then, like a leaf blown by a very sprightly wind, she whirled and twirled her way out the door and was gone.

As you might expect, Mike now had a special impetus to find me and talk. He beat feet over to Madonna house, burst in, and told me the whole story.

I exclaimed, "This is unreal!"

I couldn't wait to find out more. So the next morning, when Sister Agnes called me in my office and said, "Mother wants to see you," she didn't have to ask twice. I was out the door and over to the convent next to the studio in the blink of an eye.

I walked over to the parlor next to the cloister where the nuns live. Here, through a window with bars on it, visitors could meet with the nuns and talk. However, today, the whole parlor on the nuns' side of the bars was packed to the rafters with nuns! And no wonder, because there was Mother Angelica in the midst of them, standing without braces or crutches or even a little support from the other sisters. As I walked in, she looked at me with all the giggly giddiness of a young girl I was picking up for the prom. She twirled around a time or two and her habit floated gracefully like Deborah Kerr's dress in *The King and I*. Then she said, "Well? What do you think?"

I was still adjusting to the surprise of coming down to the parlor and talking with her (normally we met in her office). Now, seeing *this* after all the decades of pain she had endured, I was overwhelmed. She came over to the bars and I kissed her on the cheek. Then I exclaimed, "Mother, this is tremendous! This is a healing for everyone! People are going to look at you and be so encouraged!"

She danced several more steps and all the nuns clapped. Everyone's faces were glowing. Sister Mary Raphael, the Mother Vicar, was so excited! Then, Sister Agnes yelled out, "Jeff! You think Mother can be on your show tonight?"

I said, "The whole *network* is Mother's! If she wants to be on my show tonight that's fine with me!" So I turned to Mother and said, "Mother, you want to be my guest tonight?"

She replied, "Yes! I want to show the *world* what God has done!"

So we prepared that day for Mother to come on. That night, the studio was absolutely packed. Word had already spread around Birmingham about Mother's healing and there was a palpable buzz in the air. Mother stood out of view with several of the nuns and, just a few seconds before air time, she handed me her crutches.

The countdown began, the cameras rolled, and I said to the television audience, "Yesterday, one of the nuns at the monastery was wearing these and today she's not. We're going to find out who, next." Then we cut to the opening theme song. The phone banks for EWTN lit up like Christmas trees! We had a record number of phone calls that night from all over the world. Then, when the theme song was done, I said, "I'd like to introduce to you all, Mother Angelica."

She came bounding out of the wings and up onto the set. Then, (as was by now becoming her custom) she grabbed me and started dancing. Then, it suddenly hit me: it was years earlier at the radio station in North Dakota that I was *dancing with nuns*! What a weird and funny foreshadow, I thought. I chuckled and wondered, "Maybe someday Kevin Costner will make a movie called *Dances with Nuns*."

So there I was, on national live television dancing with Mother Angelica, which is not an opportunity most people get. (Later on, somebody asked me, "What did you say when she said she wanted to dance with you?" I said, "What do you *say* when Mother Angelica says 'I want to dance'? You *dance!*") It was a moment of extraordinary joy and wonder and one which gave not only me, but millions of other people, a sign of hope and renewed faith that God is a living God who is still at work in the world, healing and changing lives today.

The days and weeks at EWTN were very different after that night. It was the little things that told the story of the big thing God had done. For instance, for years you could always hear Mother approaching. The "clack clack" of her braces on the linoleum floors was audible a long way off. Now, we teased her that she could sneak up on us when we were goofing off. For weeks after her healing, the staff at EWTN would still pause in the middle of conversations as Mother walked by and just stare at her. Nobody could believe it. But there it was. Our God still works wonders.

And nobody should know that better than me, since God has done so many wonderful things on my behalf without my deserving them in the slightest. And so I aim to spend the rest of my life thanking God in my family, in my work, and in those God sends me.

Looking back, I realize, of course, that the Lord God is the ultimate reason anyone becomes Catholic. Enjoying his fellowship today is not the result of anything I have done or deserve; it's all grace. Even the ability to say "yes" to his eternal proposition is a gift from God. As St. Thomas says, the "desire to be happy is not a matter of free choice."[2] "By nature the creature endowed with reason wishes to be happy."[3] Likewise I know that the life, example, and writings of Pope John Paul II played a huge role in my return to the Church as well. Of course, the faithfulness of my parents played an important role also. My father is, for me, an example of great faithfulness. He is a hard worker, a selfless man, who is always looking out for his family. Likewise, looking back now, I see the faithfulness of my mother who prayed for me at every Mass, lifting me up to the throne of God, and asking Him to bring me home. As well, I am profoundly grateful for my wife Emily. Not only did she give me a hunger for the Lord when I was eighteen years old, not only did she and her family introduce me to the Lord and show me how to read Scripture for the first time, but throughout the years she has remained steadfastly faithful to me and stuck with me during those times when I would charge off into unknown territory to see God in

---

[2] St. Thomas Aquinas, *Summa Theologiae*, I, 19, 10.
[3] St. Thomas Aquinas, *Summa Contra Gentiles*, 4, 92.

deeper ways. Marriage to a seeker isn't always easy, but Emily was always behind me saying, "Where are we going now?" She has had a marvelous attitude of wanting to seek the Lord *with* me through the whole thing, even though there were a few times where it was difficult for her. So a huge share of my gratitude belongs to my father, mother, and wife. In their faithfulness to pray for me, to be examples to me, to strengthen me, God gave me grace that transcends words.

In addition, of course, I also owe a huge and unpayable debt to Bishops Driscoll, McDonald, Dudley, and Carlson. To Bishop Dudley in particular, I owe thanks for counseling with me, praying for me, and supporting me from the time I was a little boy. He truly is a father in the Faith. In addition, I owe an incalculable debt to the great Thomas Howard, and to the friendship and prayers of Scott and Kimberly Hahn. Moreover, I owe a huge debt to the challenges and clarity of Karl Keating and James Akin of Catholic Answers. I am grateful for the encouragement and hope afforded by the many converts and reverts to the Church who contributed their stories to Patrick Madrid's invaluable book, *Surprised by Truth*, and for the courage and luminous insights of Blessed John Henry Cardinal Newman. Likewise, I have been profoundly nourished by the beauty of the Catholic Church shown me in the works of St. Augustine, St. Bonaventure, St. Thomas Aquinas, Karl Adam, Louis Bouyer, G. K. Chesterton, Yves Congar, Henri de Lubac, James Cardinal Gibbons, Romano Guardini, Joseph Cardinal Ratzinger, and Frank Sheed. Over and over, what comes home to me is how our life in Christ is a family affair and how much I owe to those who have gone before me.

But, in addition, I realize the past must always be the

prelude. As St. Paul says, the main thing is to "press on toward the goal of the prize of the upward call of God in Christ Jesus" (Philippians 3:14). So as I look backward with gratitude I also look forward with excitement for what God has in store and to growing in that Christian fellowship that was so badly damaged by my rebellion.

All our guesses about the future must, of course, remain mere guesses. For my own part, I know what I plan to do, subject to the Lord's approval or veto: I plan to continue with television and speaking; to do more writing; to become more involved in working with the poor; to do leadership training in my home parish; and to continue working with an exciting new ministry, Catholic Exchange (www.catholicexchange.com), a Catholic Internet portal dedicated to applying technology to facilitate evangelization and the global distribution of Christian resources, products, and services. Our intention is first to reach out to Catholics, then all other Christians, and then people from all walks of life who care about faith matters, family life, and the renewal of culture and society. To that end, Scott Hahn and I are, once again, collaborating to create *Catholic Scripture Study*, an interactive Internet feature that includes Bible studies, materials for family nights, and a question-and-answer feature called *Truth Tracts*. Also in the pipeline are several more projects utilizing various other media. In addition, we are distributing brief Scripture meditations called *Words of Encouragement* to an exponentially growing audience.

And, of course, I continue to be interested in trying to speak about the healing power of God's love to those who are, as I was, estranged from the Catholic Church. To that end, I'm now working on a book called *I'm Not Being Fed: The #1 Catholic Eating Disorder*. It will try to give some biblical and practical help to Catholics who think, as I once did, that they have to leave the Catholic Church in order to find spiritual nourishment and it will try to help the struggling Catholic see the rich banquet God has prepared for us in His Holy Catholic Church and, in particular, in the Eucharist. So life is shaping up to be both busy and productive, God willing.

But more important to me than all this is the fact that I plan on spending more time with my family. That is why Emily and I moved back to Minnesota in August 1999. My daughter Carly has, thanks be to God, been a beautiful sign of grace to me. Her ability to trust her parents' spiritual insight and her sense of adventure are wonderful. And equally wonderful are the two children Emily and I have adopted and who have become Carly's younger sisters. Jacqueline Joy ("Jaki") and Antonia Teresa ("Toni") are, as of this writing, three and one. We were there at the hospital for their births and we adopted them shortly thereafter. Like Carly, they fill my heart with joy and, as a kind of bonus, they have taught me an essential lesson of my heavenly Father's love for me. For knowing that I have been adopted into the family of God, I now get a glimpse of His divine love and care for me in the love Emily and I have for our girls. The older I get, the more I'm realizing that this is truly where my calling is: to be a father, a husband, and a holy man. More than anything else, I want to know the love of God and come to know Jesus intimately because I know I'm created in His image. So the more I get to know Him, the more I will come to know who I am and what I am called to.

Finally, in closing, let me say this. There are a lot of people who left the Catholic Church in the '70s and '80s. Some of them joined independent charismatic movements, some various other Evangelical or fundamentalist churches where they're doing great things. But there are also a lot of people I know out there who are hungry for the fullness of the Faith. If there is someone like that in your life, please don't stop praying for them. They may seem hardened, bitter, confused, or uninterested. But I bear living witness to the fact that our God remains a God who "seeks man out, moved by His fatherly heart." If we will love and pray for those who have left the Church, I believe that He Who sought me out, healed my wounds, and fed me from His banquet table can make them happy as well.

Likewise, if you are estranged from the Church for whatever reason and seeking a way back, please know that the door is open for you too. For the truth is that none of us have "arrived" in this life. We are all "searching in St. Hubert's" and asking, "When shall I come and behold the face of God?" (Psalm 42:2). If you are asking that question in the depth of your soul like the psalmist, I implore you: come Home. The sanctuary lamp that burned like a beacon so many years for me, burns also for you. Then with the grace that comes from the sacraments, and especially the Eucharist, let us all continue on this great adventure until the day we shall see Him face to face.

Postscript

After the first printing of *My Life On The Rock*, it became apparent from readers' comments that many who were excited about the Catholic Faith had a natural desire to share the Faith with others but did not know how. It is one thing to come to an understanding of the deposit of faith and to accept and begin to live it. It is quite another thing to communicate that faith to others. For some — those persistent souls whose desire for spiritual truth compels them to investigate — coming into the Catholic Church was the result of long study, digging through the Church Fathers, poring over many Church documents, tapping the depths of the Catechism and Bible. However, for others, their introduction to the Catholic Faith and their initial hunger to know more came from someone who provided a personal witness of the beauty and depth of the Faith.

I decided to add another chapter to the book to aid those who wish to engage in evangelization. The following new chapter was originally a small booklet written by my good friend Dr. Scott Hahn (who also served as a Protestant pastor before becoming Catholic) and myself that describes the process of leading others to Christ. I say "a process" because that is exactly what receiving Christ is, a process that is in many ways analogous to that followed by a couple who wish to marry.

My hope is that the combination of *My Life On The Rock* and the following section ("First Comes Love. . .") will help to equip you in understanding the process of conversion and to give you a plan to introduce friends and family to Jesus Christ and His Church.

May God bless you as you now turn your attention to the subject of evangelization, and may He be praised by all the people you encounter.

First Comes Love. . .

Leading Others to Christ

In the past few years, we have seen a real renaissance in lay Catholics who are interested in learning and defending our Faith, to offer reasoned response to common fallacies, misperceptions, and even falsehoods perpetuated about it in our culture. Yet, curiously, though we are learning to *defend* our faith, we are often still not sure how to *share* it or lead someone to a relationship with Christ. We are learning more and more what we believe and why; we are learning how to counter arguments from various quarters against it; but we still feel a bit confused when it comes to simply sharing the good news of Jesus with somebody. In a funny way we are often more comfortable with people who *don't* want to be Catholic than with people who might want to be.

Part of the reason is that Catholics know you don't just sit down, say the "sinner's prayer" and wham! you're saved. There is a whole process for becoming Catholic that includes Baptism, Confirmation, Eucharist and introduction into the sacramental and liturgical life and teaching of the Church. And so we lay Catholics are somewhat fuzzy on the role we can or should play in this process. Do you give your friends books and/or other educational materials? How do you share the faith with them and then bring them to a decision to give their lives to Christ? Is it okay for a Catholic to pray with someone to "receive Jesus"? Are we short-circuiting the journey to Baptism by doing this? On the one hand, we do not want to give our inquiring friend an overly simple idea of the Catholic Faith. On the other hand, we are uncomfortable with the idea of just handing off to a priest or Rite of Christian Initiation for Adults (RCIA) team some close friend who wants to know about the Church. How do we lay Catholics share our faith with someone in a way that respects the Church's process of initiation into the Faith and yet also respects our right and duty as laypeople to bear witness to the gospel?

Happily, we don't have to remain confused. But in order to come to the light about how to help someone become a Catholic, we must first have a clear idea of what the process of "becoming Catholic" looks like. The *Catechism of the Catholic Church* (CCC) gives us the basic outline of that process in paragraph 1229:

> From the time of the apostles, becoming a Christian has been accomplished by a journey and initiation in several stages. This journey can be covered rapidly or slowly, but certain essential elements will always have to be present: [1] proclamation of the Word, [2] acceptance of the Gospel entailing conversion, [3] profession of faith, [4] Baptism itself, the outpouring of the Holy Spirit, and admission to Eucharistic communion.

The key thing to note is that growth in faith is an *ongoing process*, not a one-time experience. It leads up to, but also goes through and beyond, Baptism. In that sense, it is very much like another human experience: the experience of courtship, engagement, and marriage. The sacraments, like the charms of the beloved, act as magnets inviting catechumens through the rites of RCIA on to communion.

When people respond to this invitation, they enter into this journey of several stages and discover the truth encapsulated in John 1:12 "But to all who received him, who believed in his name, he gave power to become children of God." However, that invitation and that response do not happen in a vacuum. In this chapter we want to underline the point that, historically, conversion to Christ has always been a process that an individual goes through within the community of the Church. While salvation is certainly a very personal experience, it is and always has been a community-based experience involving our extended spiritual family.

Courtship

The process, as CCC 1229 shows, always entails four essential elements. The first two of these are what the *Catechism* refers to as "proclamation of the Word" and "acceptance of the Gospel." This phase of the process may be called, for our purposes, *courtship*. At this phase, much of our dawning relationship with Jesus is particularly based on our own needs. We say, "I need this relationship. There has been a hole in my life. I need the Lord." Because of this, there can often be a "one-on-one" quality to the way we regard our relationship with him. That is why we call this period of conversion the courtship phase. As in any process of falling in love or developing an intense friendship, the courtship phase of conversion is that period in which a budding believer can be most deeply focused simply on "me and Jesus" just as a newly smitten lover is intensely focused

on the beloved. This will often be the case after you communicate to your friend God's deep love for us and His plan
for our life. In addition, it is during this courtship phase
that those approaching the Church often discover certain
things about themselves, but even more, they discover Jesus
and *receive* Him as John 1:12 indicates. What we discover
about ourselves during this phase is nicely summed up in
a few passages from Scripture and is precisely learned because of the "proclamation of the word." In this period,
in particular, we can facilitate this relationship with "the
proclamation of the Word" as the *Catechism* passage above
tells us. To do this, we should introduce our friend to the
beginnings of the "plan of salvation history," keeping in
mind that it is a *family* story.

First, we begin with the good news of creation: God is
not just a wise Creator, He is also our loving Father. That
is why He made us "in his own image," (Genesis 1:27) to
live as His children, by His grace. As Paul tells us in Acts
17:27–28; "He is not far from each one of us, for 'In him
we live and move and have our being' . . . 'For we are
indeed his offspring.'"

Second, God established a covenant with us from the
beginning. A covenant is a sacred family bond in which
persons give themselves to one another in loving communion. God calls us into a covenant relationship to share
friendship with Him and each other, as His family. To
keep this covenant, we must trust and obey our Father
in everything, just as we love each other as His sons and
daughters. Malachi speaks of this when he says, "Have we
not all one father? Has not one God created us? Why then
are we faithless to one another, profaning the covenant of
our fathers?" (2:10). Note how the authors of Scripture
consistently describe our relationship with God in famil-

ial and communal terms: "we," "all," "us," "one another."
Salvation is thought of in terms of "we as a family" and
"*our* Father, God."

But Malachi also laments a darker reality, crying, "Why
then are we faithless to one another, profaning the covenant
of our fathers?" This brings us to our third point: all of us
have broken God's covenant by sin. This results in more
than broken laws. It has yielded a tragic harvest of broken
lives, broken homes, and broken hearts as well throughout
society, at work and at home. As Romans 1:29–32 says in
its clear diagnosis of the human race:

> They were filled with all manner of wickedness, evil, cov-
> etousness, malice. Full of envy, murder, strife, deceit, ma-
> lignity, they are gossips, slanderers, haters of God, inso-
> lent, haughty, boastful, inventors of evil, disobedient to
> parents, foolish, faithless, heartless, ruthless. Though they
> know God's decree that those who do such things deserve
> to die, they not only do them but approve those who prac-
> tice them.

Sin bears no fruit but death, because sin kills the life of
God within us and others.

That is why we desperately need God's mercy and grace.
We like to think there is a simpler solution such as education, government, better computers or wealth. But these
solutions are just placebos for cancer. Sin's infection is too
deep and deadly. Yet, there is still hope. It is just that this
hope is not in earthly things. For our Father knows what
we need better than we do and has given us life, not in
earthly things, but in His Son Christ Jesus.

> Among these we all once lived in the passions of our flesh,
> following the desires of body and mind, and so we were
> by nature children of wrath, like the rest of mankind. But

God, who is rich in mercy, out of the great love with which he loved us, even when we were dead through our trespasses, made us alive together with Christ (by grace you have been saved), and raised us up with him, and made us sit with him in the heavenly places in Christ Jesus, that in the coming ages he might show the immeasurable riches of his grace in kindness toward us in Christ Jesus (Ephesians 2:3–7).

That is good news. And when we really lay hold of it we become fascinated by the beauty of the Gospel just as a man becomes fascinated by that special someone he would like to court. In that phase, we are especially to act as "best friends of the Groom and bride," taking a genuine interest in others, not because they are "potential converts" but because they are *precious to God*. We are interested in winning souls because *God* is interested in winning souls. Our motivation for soul winning has to be centered in God's will. So get to know the person: their family, work, and interests. Ask the Holy Spirit to empower you, to give you a love for the person, and to give you the words to speak. Remember that soul-winning is one brother or sister welcoming another sibling back into the family. We should also, as questions arise, familiarize ourselves with the teaching of the Church via the *Catechism of the Catholic Church* and other resource materials. (Don't be afraid to say those three extremely valuable words: "I don't know." Followed by, of course, "But I'll try to find out.")

In doing this, we help the person we are mentoring understand who they are in light of the Big Picture, that is, salvation history. We should address the fact that they are created in the image of someone (God) and that their search for significance, identity, and purpose ends in Christ. We should keep in mind what St. Augustine said: "You have made us for yourself, O Lord, and our hearts are restless until they rest in thee." When we lead someone to Christ during the courtship phase, it is important to show that God has an answer to our spiritual, emotional, intellectual, and physical needs. We want to show that true happiness can be found only in the Blessed Trinity. Our goal in this whole process is the realization, acknowledgement, and acceptance of the fact that we are called to divine sonship. And we will typically find a receptive audience since the words of Scripture are, to the soul disposed to receive Jesus, as the words of a love letter are to the beloved.

In addition to assisting in the proclamation of the word in everyday life, the lay Catholic can also invite a friend to pray in accord with Paul's teaching that

> If you confess with your lips that Jesus is Lord and believe in your heart that God raised him from the dead, you will be saved. For man believes with his heart and so is justified, and he confesses with his lips and so is saved. The scripture says, "No one who believes in him will be put to shame" (Romans 10:9–11).

There are two kinds of prayer to keep in mind depending on the person you are hoping to guide into the Catholic Church during the courtship phase. For the new believer who has no background in the Christian faith at all, it would be good to pray something like this:

> Dear Lord Jesus,
>
> I thank you that you love me so much that you came and died for me. I repent of walking contrary to your ways and ask you to forgive me and create in me a clean heart. I know that you are the Lord of the Universe, please come into my heart and be Lord of my life. As I begin my new walk with you I pray that I will love you more deeply

every day, evidenced by a life of obedience. As I submit myself to your family, the Church, help me to learn about you and discover my place in your body. Thank you for this new life and a chance to begin anew. In the name of the Father, the Son, and the Holy Spirit. Amen.

The second sort of prayer we need to keep in mind is for the Christian who has been baptized but has not consciously pursued a relationship with God before. A prayer aimed at renewing the graces given at baptism and seeking a fresh outpouring of the Holy Spirit might go something like this:

Dear Lord Jesus,

I thank you that you love me so much that you came and died for me. I repent of walking contrary to your ways and ask you to forgive me and create in me a clean heart. I know that you are the Lord of the Universe, please come into my heart and be Lord of my life. As I renew my walk with you I pray that I will love you more deeply every day, evidenced by a life of obedience. As I submit myself to your family, the Church, help me to learn about you and discover my place in your body. Thank you for the life you gave me at baptism and this chance to renew my relationship with you. In the name of the Father, the Son, and the Holy Spirit. Amen.

One excellent way of honoring this prayer of initial trust in Jesus would be for you to present your friend with a copy of the Bible and the *Catechism of the Catholic Church* as a sort of "marker stone" (just as the ancient Israelites used to erect stone monuments at important sites in their history). A good translation of Scripture is absolutely essential to a healthy Catholic disciple. We recommend the Revised Standard Version — Catholic edition (Scepter Press and Ignatius Press both publish this). The New American Bible is also good.

Unlike what many Protestants would contend, saying the sinner's prayer is only the *beginning* of approaching salvation and walking with Christ. This is neither a "salvation formula" nor a non-refundable, non-revocable ticket to Heaven. Saying this prayer is a bit like asking or accepting the offer for a first date. It is intended to be purposeful, it can be emotional, but it certainly is tentative and non-binding. We are telling Jesus "Yes, I am interested in beginning a journey with you." But salvation does not result from simply "dating" God. God grants us salvation through binding Himself to us in covenant. Baptism, not the "Sinner's Prayer," is that covenantal, binding power that saves.

To Catholics, much of this sounds and feels very "Protestant." And, in fact, as Protestant pastors we imagined the primary work of "becoming a Christian" was done in this phase of proclaiming the word and seeing it accepted in prayer. You sat down with somebody and within ten minutes, after a few preliminary questions, you could lead this person in the "Sinner's Prayer" and your mission was nearly complete. To be sure, the rest of their life was to be spent going to church, reading the Bible, attending home groups, etc. But people are given assurance that they have been "saved and complete" when they have prayed this prayer.

Catholics are rightly suspicious of this. From a Catholic perspective, this sort of instant Christianity lacks roots in relationship. To return to the courtship analogy, it is like saying, "Who cares about all this complicated theology of marriage and all these elaborate rules and regulations! All I know is that I love her and so we consummated our relationship on the first date." The fact is, such hasty relationships seldom last. This is why Jesus warns us against having "no root" (Matthew 13:21). One may argue that the elaborate "rules and regulations" keep people from the truth. On the contrary, one may quickly enter into a relationship with Christ based on very limited knowledge, similar to many who quickly fall in love. But the nature of relationship is such that they become more complex, deep and interesting as one learns more about the other. This is certainly true of our relationship with Christ. The mere child should be able to respond to Christ's grace, then grow in it into eternity.

On the other hand, though it is a mistake to equate courtship with *marriage*, it is not a mistake to equate courtship with *courtship*. That is, there is real value to be found in the excitement of the convert's budding relationship with Jesus Christ and it is perfectly legitimate for the Catholic to foster this by encouraging the new believer to pray to Jesus, to ask Him to be Lord and Savior, and to help this new Christian cultivate a life of personal prayer. As long as we make clear that the new believer is *embarking* on the Great Journey of Faith and has not *arrived* this is perfectly legitimate and perfectly Catholic.

One frequent characteristic of the courtship phase is often a certain "free-floating" quality to the new believer's life. We go to this meeting, we go to that meeting. We try this teacher and that teacher, this preacher and that preacher, this seminar and that conference, this parish and that parish. We sort of take Jesus with us wherever we go. We are not always thinking in terms of commitment to anybody besides Him. It can be emotionally exhilarating and adventuresome! But like courtship, it is also a phase that inexorably draws us to a choice.

Commitment

Sooner or later, in every courtship, the question inevitably arises, "Do I or do I not want to belong to this person?" There is a natural progression from courtship to this question, just as there is a natural progression in John 1:12 from "receiving" Christ to "believing in his name." If we truly want to belong to others that means we have to accept them as they are in the full complexity of their relationships with others. In the case of a human relationship between a man and a woman that involves a paradox. On the one hand, if we decide to get engaged we simultaneously commit ourselves to one another in a deeper way while at the same time opening ourselves to other family relationships that we had not even thought about before. So, for instance, when a man becomes more serious about a woman he necessarily finds himself being bound more closely to her father, mother, sisters, and brothers and friends as well. In the same way, to love Jesus presents us with the challenge and the invitation to love those He loves.

This challenge is not always met by the new believer. In many ways, Protestantism often represents a kind of shrinking from that challenge. Rather than deal with the fact that Jesus has chosen to associate Himself with quite a diverse collection of people who are not always to our taste, Protestantism can often be in reality the attempt to run away to Vegas with Jesus and ignore His family. This is commonly referred to as eloping, celebrating the marriage alone without those who are particularly meaningful to either the Bride or Groom. Hence the many appeals to the "invisible Church" (so much more easy to stomach than the real Christian with the irritating wheeze in the pew next to you) and the avoidance of Mary, the saints, (and the sinners) who are the family of Jesus.

Given the reality of Jesus' relationship with other members of His family, it is very important for the Catholic mentor to emphasize the necessity of real faithfulness and discipleship in the commitment phase of a new believer's life in Christ. If the need for this is communicated successfully, then the new believer will begin to see that he can derive more from his relationship with Jesus by assuming the posture of learner rather than that of a critic or gourmet.

It is in this phase that it is wise for the new believer to enroll in the catechumenate process, which is the beginning of the initiation into the sacramental and liturgical life of the Church. Just as engagement is a deeper commitment than courtship, yet not as deep as full entry into married life, so the catechumenate is an expression of deeper commitment that is nonetheless still a journey in process and not the fullness of sacramental grace given in Baptism. Catechumens going through such a process can benefit immeasurably from the help and guidance of experienced Catholics.

> Catechumens "are already joined to the Church, they are already of the household of Christ, and are quite frequently already living a life of faith, hope and charity." "With love and solicitude mother Church already embraces them as her own" (CCC 1249).

During this period, therefore, lay Catholics in particular can be extremely valuable in acting as sponsors and mentors for those entering the Church.

In addition, we can be of great assistance by continuing

to show the progressive unfolding of the "plan of salvation history" as it leads toward the Easter mysteries. You can discuss how the solution for sin came when God became man in Jesus Christ and took on our weak and mortally wounded nature, not only to heal and perfect us, but to elevate us to share in His own life of divine sonship, to make us one with His Father. As Hebrews 2:11 says: "For he who sanctifies and those who are sanctified have all one origin. That is why he is not ashamed to call them brethren." Jesus did what no one else could do: destroyed sin at its source.

> Since therefore the children share in flesh and blood, he himself likewise partook of the same nature, that through death he might destroy him who has the power of death, that is, the devil, and deliver all those who through fear of death were subject to lifelong bondage (Hebrews 2:14–15).

Through His suffering and death, we are healed and brought home. Encourage your friend with the confidence and hope of 1 John 3:1: "See what love the Father has given us, that we should be called children of God; and so we are."

Also, as you move toward the Easter mysteries, discuss the reality that Jesus seals the New Covenant with us through His self-offering. This sacrifice began in the Upper Room, at the Passover meal, when He said to His disciples: " 'Take, eat; this is my body.' And he took a cup, and when he had given thanks he gave it to them, saying, 'Drink of it, all of you; for this is my blood of the covenant, which is poured out for many for the forgiveness of sins' " (Matthew 26:26–28). Christ sacrificed Himself for us, first by instituting the Eucharist, and then by dying for us on

Calvary. Discuss with your friend the indivisible unity of this entire action of Christ helping to ready him to participate in the coming Easter mysteries.

Finally, it is essential to discuss with your friend the reality that Jesus was raised from the dead by the power of the Holy Spirit and that He gives this same Spirit to us as His gift. "And because you are sons, God has sent the Spirit of his Son into our hearts, crying, 'Abba! Father!'" (Galatians 4:6). God promises to give the Spirit to all who ask: "If you then, who are evil, know how to give good gifts to your children, how much more will the heavenly Father give the Holy Spirit to those who ask him!" (Luke 11:13). This also is excellent preparation for the sacraments of Baptism (if your friend is unbaptized) and Confirmation. For, of course, the Holy Spirit comes to us through the sacraments in a powerful way; since Jesus instituted them, and now administers them to us, beginning with Baptism. "You were washed, you were sanctified, you were justified in the name of the Lord Jesus Christ and in the Spirit of our God" (1 Corinthians 6:11). The greatest of the seven sacraments is the Eucharist, because it is the sacrifice of the New Covenant and the family meal that nourishes us with Jesus' own Body and Blood, just as He promised: "I am the bread of life. . . my flesh is food indeed, and my blood is drink indeed. He who eats my flesh and drinks my blood abides in me, and I in him" (John 6:48, 55–56). Discuss with your friend how He calls us to share this living Bread at the Father's table. "Behold, I stand at the door and knock; if any one hears my voice and opens the door, I will come in to him and eat with him, and he with me" (Revelation 3:20).

Above all, remember that the way to communicate all this is not merely by talking, but by *doing*. History shows that people continue and mature in their faith by following the pattern of those who led them to faith. That means that in the commitment phase your friend will be watching you and learning from you. The chances are very high that the way in which you celebrate the sacraments, pray, read the Bible, and practice the Faith is the way your friend will do it too. This means you must spend time with your friend and remember what Paul said: "Be imitators of me, as I am of Christ" (1 Corinthians 11:1). It is good, both for your sake and for your friend's sake, for you to use this phase to cultivate a love for the basics of the Catholic Faith. Frequent attendance at Mass, confession, daily devotions, and cultivating virtue are all helpful in this regard. Also, helping to model a healthy respect for the apostolic authority of the Church leads to a healthy respect for Christ. The new believer must learn to hear Christ's voice in the voice of the Church.

Since this process, like the process of engagement, involves the slow unfolding of a revelation and a relationship, the Church marks this process of unfolding by means of various rites.

> This initiation has varied greatly through the centuries according to circumstances. In the first centuries of the Church, Christian initiation saw considerable development. A long period of *catechumenate* included a series of preparatory rites, which were liturgical landmarks along the path of catechumenal preparation and culminated in the celebration of the sacraments of Christian initiation (CCC 1230).

Today, the general process involves three basic rites: the Pre-Catechumenate, the Rite of Acceptance or Welcoming, and the Rites of Election (for the unbaptized) and of Continuing Conversion (for the baptized). The Pre-Catechumenate varies in length and aims to remove barriers and deliver the gospel for the first time. It is important to remember that some in the RCIA program may be there simply because they have to do so to get married. Still, they will hear the word of God and we must be an encouragement to them. The Rite of Acceptance or Welcoming has as its goal the complete conversion to adult Christian life among the catechumens. During this phase, catechumens leave Mass before Communion in order to discuss the Scripture readings. They begin to be pastored as the bishops and pope pray every day for catechumens and the RCIA team, sponsors, and priests form deeper relationships with each of the catechumens.

During this time, it is a good idea to introduce your friend to some of the Church's treasury of prayers and devotions. Many people take this time to explain the rosary, for instance and to cultivate times to pray it with the persons they are discipling. It is also a great thing for the Catholic mentor to remember that many people are embarrassed about not knowing the intricacies of the faith such as various postures and responses of the Mass, the different mysteries of the rosary and so forth. Assure them that this is okay and that they will understand it in time. Help them as they have need.

Finally, the Church celebrates the Rite of Election for the unbaptized and the Rite of Continuing Conversion for the baptized on the first Sunday of Lent. This is the only portion of the catechumenate that is on a fixed time schedule. It is a period of purification and enlightenment. In addition, the baptized go to confession.

In all this, the bride enters into a real oneness of Spirit with the Groom throughout the engagement period. The commitment grows ever deeper, but also the realization of our dependence on Jesus and our love for His family grows as well. Catechumens find increasingly that their real but immature relationship with Christ requires the help of the Church. During this phase your friend may want answers to questions concerning Mary, the papacy, confessing to a priest, the role of Scripture in the Catholic's life, the saints and Purgatory. While you may not think that these subjects are impediments to faith, they will most likely be confronted by friends or family and asked to give an explanation. Indeed, new converts or catechumens can sometimes be derailed in their faith by confusion caused by an inability to reply to these sorts of objections. Therefore, it is a good idea to become familiar with these topics so that you can engage in conversation and help clarify these Church teachings. They also find themselves discovering, not that they have "arrived" when they accepted Jesus as Lord, but rather that they are hungry for full communion with Him in the sacraments of initiation. It is, again, like the progression from first kiss to the wedding night. It involves growth, preparation, increasing self-knowledge, and ever-deepening devotion to the Groom. And this process culminates in the third step: communion.

Communion

The whole catechumenate process aims at the drama of the Triduum (Three Days) and, in particular, the Easter vigil Mass on Holy Saturday night. It is here that the catechumen receives Jesus entirely and, in the words of John 1:12, receives power to become a child of God. Many people wonder why the Church surrounds this event with such great pomp and ceremony. The reason is that we are human

and it is perfectly normal (and built into us by the Blessed
Trinity) to surround the huge events of our lives with ritual
and ceremony. This is why, when a man and woman fall
in love, we surround this mystery with enormous amounts
of ritual and ceremony to say what we cannot say with
mere words rather than simply having a bunch of people
stand around the room while the bride and groom discuss
getting an apartment together.

And that is the key to the Easter Vigil as well. For it
is a kind of marriage celebration. The catechumens are
dressed in white just like a bride, for they are to enter into
the purity of the Lamb of God Himself and partake of
the Marriage Feast of the Lamb and the abundant gifts of
His Spirit. They undergo the sacrament of Baptism, which
not only purifies them from all sin, but also makes them a
"new creature," an adopted child of God, who has become
a "partaker of the divine nature" (2 Peter 1:4). In addition,
Baptism "marks" us and makes us members of the Body
of Christ. That is, we become members (the term means
"body parts"), not only of Christ, but of *one another* (Romans 12:5). The family of the Groom becomes *our* family and the gifts He gives us are intended to be shared
with each other so that the whole family will be blessed
(1 Corinthians 12; Romans 12). Moreover, by Baptism we
share in Christ's offices of Priest, Prophet, and King and
are empowered by His Spirit to take up His mission in
union with the family of God that is the Church.

To fully participate in that mission, we need the help of
the second of the sacraments of initiation: Confirmation.
This sacrament is, in particular, the sacrament of friendship
with God where we receive the full outpouring of the Holy
Spirit and His gifts, empowering us to act as ambassadors
for Christ.

Like Baptism which it completes, Confirmation is given only once, for it too imprints on the soul an *indelible spiritual mark*, the "character," which is the sign that Jesus Christ has marked a Christian with the seal of his Spirit by clothing him with power from on high so that he may be his witness.

This "character" perfects the common priesthood of the faithful, received in Baptism, and "the confirmed person receives the power to profess faith in Christ publicly and as it were officially" (CCC 1304–1305).

And so, "having become a child of God clothed with the wedding garment, the neophyte . . . receives the food of the new life, the body and blood of Christ" (CCC 1244). Everything leads up to the greatest of the sacraments of initiation, Holy Eucharist. Here, at last, is the moment we have waited for: our participation in the Marriage Supper of the Lamb (Revelation 19:9).

> The Eucharist is "the source and summit of the Christian life. The other sacraments, are indeed all ecclesiastical ministries and works of the apostolate, are bound up with the Eucharist and are oriented toward it. For in the blessed Eucharist is contained the whole spiritual good of the Church, namely Christ himself, our Pasch [Passover]" (CCC 1324).

Here is the mystery of total mutual self-giving experienced completely. Jesus Christ, fully God and fully man, gives Himself completely to us — Body, Blood, soul, and divinity — in the mystery of the Holy Eucharist just as the Groom gives Himself completely to the Bride in self-sacrificial love. Likewise, we offer ourselves to Him upon the altar in the Mass and are taken up into the Blessed life of the Trinity through His self-offering to God. Once again, we see this strange and wonderful way in which the sacraments of the Eucharist and Matrimony are beautifully related in just the way that Paul describes in Ephesians 5:21–32, a passage which concludes:

> "For this reason a man shall leave his father and mother and be joined to his wife, and the two shall become one flesh." This mystery is a profound one, and I am saying that it refers to Christ and the Church.

Since Baptism really is a kind of wedding, it is appropriate to speak of the period after Baptism as a sort of Honeymoon. And, indeed, the Church begins what is called the "neophyte year" in which the newly baptized are to continue learning and living the Faith in communion, not only with the Groom, but with the Groom's family, the Church. We are to discover the reality of our common brotherhood in Christ. Also, we are to discover more deeply our union in the Eucharist, our fellowship with our mother Mary (John 19:26–27) and the saints (Hebrews 12:1), and the fullness of the Tradition preserved by the Church which is the "pillar and bulwark of the truth" (1 Timothy 3:15) as it is guided by the successor of Peter, the pope (Matthew 16:18). To that end, all the Scripture readings for the next seven weeks after Easter are aimed primarily at the neophyte. And this brings us to the final opportunity we as lay Catholics have for sharing our faith. It is generally estimated that as many as one half of the people who enter the Church through the RCIA process in the United States are not practicing the Faith after the first year, due to a combination of poor catechesis and a lack of relationship with members of the parish at a personal level. That is, about half the people who enter the Church at Easter are gone by the following Easter. Why? Nobody was there to help them get connected at the parish or "hold fast the traditions" (2 Thessalonians 2:15) or give them a sense of what they were doing now that they were flopping around on the shores of the vast Catholic Ocean. We, as lay people, have primary responsibility to make sure that this does not happen.

Therefore, once Easter is past, it is critical that we continue to help our friend to become rooted in the family of God. We must show that the Catholic Church is God's worldwide family that the Father sent the Son to establish by the Spirit. "That they may all be one; even as thou, Father, art in me, and I in thee, that they also may be in us, so that the world may believe that thou hast sent me" (John 17:21). So we love the Church as our mother, revere it as Christ's Bride and obey its teachings, all because we trust that Jesus will be true to His word: "And I tell you, you are Peter, and on this rock I will build my church, and the powers of death shall not prevail against it" (Matthew 16:18). We must also show our friend that Jesus doesn't stop there; He also gives us His mother, Mary, to be our own spiritual mother. "When Jesus saw his mother, and the disciple whom he loved standing near, he said to his mother, 'Woman, behold, your son!' Then he said to the disciple, 'Behold, your mother!'" (John 19:26–27; see Revelation 12:1–2, 5, 17). Mary's grace all comes from Jesus. That is what makes her so powerful in God's family. No one ever honored His mother like Jesus; now He wants us to imitate Him.

Further, we must make clear that the Christian life has a point, purpose, and goal in eternity. For as God's children, we are not simply people wandering around "practicing random acts of kindness and senseless beauty." We are earthly pilgrims heading home to Heaven. This makes

Heaven our true homeland, and death the true homecoming! "But our commonwealth is in heaven, and from it we await a Savior, the Lord Jesus Christ, who will change our lowly body to be like His glorious body, by the power which enables him even to subject all things to himself" (Philippians 3:20–21). In the angels and saints who have gone before us are older brothers and sisters. "But you have come to Mount Zion and to the city of the living God, the heavenly Jerusalem, and to innumerable angels in festal gathering, and to the assembly of the first-born who are enrolled in heaven, and to a judge who is God of all, and to the spirits of just men made perfect" (Hebrews 12:22–23).

Emphasize to your friend that to know God is to have a relationship with God. The Hebrew word for "know" is *da'at*, which implies relationship. We know God, because we relate to Him on an ongoing basis. Faithfulness, both in the area of ongoing learning and obeying is critical for a long happy life with God. Assist your friend in developing testimony to share with others. God expects new converts not to retire, but to be witnesses and to make disciples themselves. Pray for your friend daily. Remember that a changed heart is achieved only by the grace of God.

In summary, there are many ways in which we as lay Catholics can share our faith in Christ as new believers make the journey from courtship to commitment to communion and on through the honeymoon to full life in Christ. Our prayers, commitment, friendship, discipleship, and love can very often be a major and even central source of sustenance for the new Catholic. So by all means get involved in your parish's RCIA program and get to know catechumens and newly baptized members. Befriend them. Find ways in which their gifts, talents, and interests can be linked to needs in the parish or the community. Help them to make connections with others in the parish who may enjoy their friendship. Spend time with them. Do not for a moment think that you have no role to play in bringing new Catholics into the Faith. It may well be that, for more people than you realize, you are the only Jesus they have ever met. Take hold of the gifts that you yourself have received in Baptism, Confirmation, and Eucharist and be the ambassador for Christ that God has called you to be. With the help of His Holy Spirit and His Holy Catholic Church, you can do greater things than you have ever imagined.

—Jeff Cavins and Dr. Scott Hahn

Recommended Reading

By What Authority? An Evangelical Discovers Tradition, Mark Shea (Our Sunday Visitor).

A Catechesis on the Creed Volumes I–V, Pope John Paul II (Pauline Books & Media).

Catholic and Christian, Alan Schreck (Servant).

Catholicism and Fundamentalism, Karl Keating (Ignatius Press).

Catholic for a Reason: Scripture and the Mystery of the Family of God, Leon Suprenant, Scott Hahn, et al. (Emmaus Road).

Crossing the Tiber, Stephen K. Ray (Ignatius Press).

Evangelical Is Not Enough, Thomas Howard (Ignatius Press).

A Father Who Keeps His Promises, Scott Hahn (Servant).

The Fathers of the Church, Mike Aquilina (Our Sunday Visitor).

The Lamb's Supper, Scott Hahn (Doubleday).

Making Senses Out of Scripture, Mark Shea (Basilica Press).

On Being Catholic, Thomas Howard (Ignatius Press).

Pope Fiction, Patrick Madrid (Basilica Press).

Rome Sweet Home, Scott and Kimberly Hahn (Ignatius Press).

Surprised by Truth: 11 Converts Give the Biblical and Historical Reasons for Becoming Catholic, Patrick Madrid (Basilica Press).

Theology and Sanity, Frank Sheed (Ignatius Press).

Theology for Beginners, Frank Sheed (Servant).

Upon This Rock, Stephen K. Ray (Ignatius Press).